WITH DEA

Famed for its nationwide coverage of crime and punishment, *Court TV* is <u>the</u> source for the most up-to-date, in-depth, on-the-scene true crime reporting. Now, for the millions of fans of the acclaimed series, *Crime Stories,* comes the shocking facts about today's most sensational trials.

"THE HOG TRAIL MURDERS"—Port Charlotte, Florida's, Hog Trail area was a broad belt of densely wooded land good for hunting fierce, tusked, wild hogs. When the mutilated bodies of nameless men were found there, police went hunting for a dangerous, two-legged killer.

"PRESCRIPTION FOR MURDER"—Port St. Lucie, Florida, residents were shocked when elderly Mollie Frazier was attacked and beaten to death. There were more shocked when the killer's defense team blamed it all on anti-depressant medication.

"THE SCOUTMASTER'S SECRET"—Lonoke, Arkansas. No one knew the scoutmaster was a child molester except the boys in his troop . . . Until Eagle Scout Heath Stocks gunned down his parents and sister.

With 16 pages of exclusive photos provided by *Court TV*!

BOOK YOUR PLACE ON OUR WEBSITE AND MAKE THE READING CONNECTION!

We've created a customized website just for our very special readers, where you can get the inside scoop on everything that's going on with Zebra, Pinnacle and Kensington books.

When you come online, you'll have the exciting opportunity to:

- View covers of upcoming books
- Read sample chapters
- Learn about our future publishing schedule (listed by publication month *and author*)
- Find out when your favorite authors will be visiting a city near you
- Search for and order backlist books from our online catalog
- Check out author bios and background information
- Send e-mail to your favorite authors
- Meet the Kensington staff online
- Join us in weekly chats with authors, readers and other guests
- Get writing guidelines
- AND MUCH MORE!

**Visit our website at
http://www.kensingtonbooks.com**

CRIME STORIES:
THE BEST OF *COURT TV*

WITH DEADLY INTENT

David Jacobs

PINNACLE BOOKS
Kensington Publishing Corp.

http://www.pinnaclebooks.com

PINNACLE BOOKS are published by

Kensington Publishing Corp.
850 Third Avenue
New York, NY 10022

All Kensington Titles, Imprints, and Distributed Lines are
available at special quantity discounts for bulk purchases
for sales promotion, premiums, fund-raising, and educa-
tional or institutional use. Special book excerpts or customized printings can also be created to fit specific needs.
For details, write or phone the office of the Kensington
special sales manager: Kensington Publishing Corp., 850
Third Avenue, New York, NY 10022, attn: Special Sales
Department, Phone: 1-800-221-2647.

Pinnacle and the P logo Reg. U.S. Pat. & TM Off.

First Printing: November 2001
10 9 8 7 6 5 4 3 2 1

Printed in the United States of America

CONTENTS

Florida v. *Conahan:*

"The Hog Trail Murders"

The Crime

Florida, the Sunshine State, has experienced many boom-and-bust development cycles. One such took place just inland of the central southwest coast, along the Highway 41 corridor running through Charlotte and Lee counties, from Punta Gorda south to Fort Myers. During the boom, planned housing tracts were laid out along the highway, and a street grid was put into place. But the promoters and developers went bust and the planned tracts were never developed. Brush came back, reclaiming cleared lots, swallowing up the subdivisions, leaving a broad belt of woods now used mainly as dumping grounds.

The area attracted wild hogs—the fierce, gnarly, belligerent cousins of the more domesticated and detusked farm porkers. Wild boars are always a good indication of sparse human population. Hunters frequented the area, hunting the boars, causing the zone to be known as the Hog Trails. It was good country for dumping trash, wild hog hunting, and engaging in clandestine sexual encounters with male and female prostitutes. A perfect place for a murder.

On February 1, 1994, in north Port Charlotte, in a wooded Hog Trail area off Biscayne Boulevard, a citizen driving along a dirt road noticed a flock of buzzards circling the area. Buzzards meant carrion. Thinking it was roadkill, a deer or hog, the man stopped to investigate. He wanted a hog skull it would make a nice offbeat decoration for his home. He got out of his vehicle to take a look around. A path led through dense woods, suddenly opening up into a wide spacious area under a canopy of trees. There lay a dead body.

Later at the scene, police observed that the cadaver was that of a male, lying on his back, positioned as if being displayed. The body had been there from two to four weeks. There were no clothes, nor identification. Florida is rough on bodies, and the corpse had suffered from rapid decomposition, exposure to heat, rain, insects and wild animals. The lower part of the jaw was missing, and animals had dragged some of the bones under the palmetto bushes, gnawing them clean.

The body's genitals were missing, but not because of the depredations of any four-legged animals. They'd been cut out. The body was that of a victim, posed by a killer who'd excised the genitals and taken them away. The killer seemed to have policed the crime scene, sanitizing it of possible evidence.

Charlotte County Sheriff's Office Detective Rick Hobbs, working the scene, uncovered grooves worn into some tree trunks, ligature or rope marks caused perhaps by the victim being bound to a tree. The missing jawbone was found under some bushes. The missing genitals were not found.

The victim was labeled "John Doe." In the months ahead, as the body count mounted, he would instead come to be known as "John Doe Number One."

On March 5, 1995, at a Fort Myers park that was a known haunt of male prostitutes, a blue Mercury Capri pulled up alongside self-described "street hustler" David Payton. Payton was called over to the car by the driver, a middle-aged white man who asked him if he wanted to "get high." The driver was burly, about forty, soft spoken and unassuming. Payton got in and the car drove away.

While they drove, the driver gave Payton beer, Valium, and marijuana. Payton got "pretty high." Woozy, several times he felt on the verge of passing out, though he wasn't so far gone that he didn't notice the driver trying to slip more Valium into his beer.

The driver asked Payton if he would be interested in posing for nude pictures for money. Payton said he might be interested. The man asked Payton if he could tie him to a tree and photograph him. Payton started to get a little bit worried.

They were in South Punta Gorda, on Zemel Road, somewhere out in the boondocks. The car followed a dirt road leading to a remote wooded area used as a dumping ground. That wass where they'd take the pictures.

Along the way, there was a minor mishap as the car drove into a pothole and got stuck. The area was remote, but not that remote. Before too long, another vehicle came along, its two occupants stopping to give assistance. They were hog hunters.

The samaritans offered to help push the car out of the hole. Payton started to get out, to help push. The Capri driver's demeanor changed drastically, almost a Jekyll-and-Hyde transformation. No longer mild-mannered and accommodating, he became assured, authoritative, domineering. He pushed Payton back into the seat cushion, saying, "I'll get out."

The driver got out leaving Payton to steer while the others hefted the car out of the hole. As they were getting into position, Payton had a spare moment or two to look around the vehicle. In the backseat was a sack containing a Polaroid camera, some rope, a blue tarp, and a knife.

Payton had the thought that maybe the driver

hadn't wanted him to get out because he didn't want the hunters to be able to identify Payton later.

Outside, the others were ready to free the car. Payton sat in the driver's seat, as the trio lifted and pushed the car while he gave it the gas.

The car lurched forward out of the hole, free. Payton kept his foot on the gas and just kept on going, driving away, swiftly leaving the other three far behind, then losing them entirely.

In a haze from the booze, pills, and weed, Payton somehow managed to find his way out of the Hog Trails and onto paved roads. Along the way, he drifted out, losing consciousness entirely.

He awoke, confused, thinking that he was back in his own bedroom. Only what were all those cops doing there?

Fully awake now, he realized that he was still in the car, stalled at some intersection's stop sign where he'd passed out sitting behind the wheel, foot on the brake pedal.

Payton was arrested and charged with auto theft. The car was registered to Daniel Conahan, Sr., a retired elderly man from Punta Gorda, who said he'd lent the car to his son. To the police, it was an open-and-shut case. Nobody believed Payton's story that he'd stolen the car out of fear for his life, fear that he'd be murdered. It sounded like just another lame excuse from a perp who'd been caught red-handed with the goods, and Payton went to prison for grand theft auto.

A year or so later, though, it didn't sound so farfetched. Payton was a member of a very exclusive club: those who'd gone off into the woods with the Hog Trail killer and returned to tell the tale.

Most dogs like to dig up stuff and bring it home, and Hollywood was no exception. Home was a stilt house in the Northport Estates area. Hog Trail woods lay nearby and the dog was constantly bringing home bones, among them those of possums, hogs, deer, alligators, raccoons, etc.

On January 1, 1996, New Year's Day, Hollywood's owner came out of his house to find the dog chewing on a human skull. He called the police, who formed up a search party and went to work searching for the rest of the remains.

Leading the investigation was Northport Police Department Detective Tom Choiniere who later told *Court TV,* "Some days you'll come in and be doing mundane, routine things and the next moment you're getting a call that this guy's dog brought somebody's head home and it's in his front yard. You just never know."

The abandoned street grid helped in the search, making the remote area accessible, dividing it up into sectors cordoned off for block-by-block searches. The brush was thick and tough, often requiring cutting by machetes to make any progress. Searchers had to go where animals could go, which meant going under brush. They used horses, dogs, and volunteers. Sanitation workers and construction workers pitched in.

A few days later, they found the rest of the remains, at a site about a quarter mile from the house, in the woods off Plamendon Street in Northport. The body lay on its back, naked, arms at its sides, legs slightly spread apart. Posed. Most of the skeleton was intact. Enough skin remained to yield some partial fingerprints and palm prints. Forensics determined that the deceased had been a "large, large-boned, white male, possibly of Eastern Block or Slavic denomination, Polish, Czechoslovakian, six-two to six-five and possibly well over two hundred pounds."

One thing more: the victim had had bad teeth. Another nameless body. Another John Doe.

On March 7, 1996, in Northport, south of the interstate highway, off Toledo Blade Boulevard on Laramie Circle, a passing motorist pulled off to the side of the road to relieve himself. He went into the woods and noticed a smell. Looking up, he saw a body lying nearby on the ground. He got back in his car, driving to a Pick and Run store, where he used a pay phone to call 911.

Beyond dense woods, in the open under a tree canopy, surrounded by a mix of cabbage palm and pineapple palm trees, police found the corpse. Insect infestation was fairly well advanced, as was decomposition. The naked body lay on its back, posed, with his genitals cut off. Apart from that, it was largely intact. The body also bore knife wounds.

An officer noticed ligature marks on a nearby tree, where the victim had been tied to it. The marks corresponded to the victim's leg, waist, and neck areas. Tellingly, there were no marks on the tree where the victim would have been leaning against it, because he'd been between the tree and the ropes.

An autopsy revealed that the victim had been dead for about a week to ten days. Ligature marks on the neck indicated that he'd been strangled, but not to death. For some reason, the killer had been unable to finish strangling him. He'd been stabbed four times, and that was what killed him.

The medical examiner found during the autopsy that the victim had striation marks across his shins, possible rope burns. Also, there were vertical cuts across his thighs, shins, and the bottoms of his feet. They may have been cuts inflicted by the razor-sharp edges of palmetto bushes at the crime scene. That suggested that the victim had gotten free from his bonds and run away, trying to escape. The cuts were consistent with the kind of wounds he would have sustained during his short, wild, desperate flight. His assailant had caught him and fatally stabbed him.

Until the finding of March 7, 1996, police had made no connection between the Port Charlotte John Doe and Northport's John Doe. Now, though, Detective Tom Choiniere believed that the two Northport homicides were the work of the same individual. So did Charlotte County Sheriff's Office Detective Rick Hobbs, investigating the Port Charlotte John Doe found in February 1994. He contacted Choiniere, noting the similarities between the three cases.

As the Port Charlotte body was the first found, he was officially John Doe Number One. The first Northport body became John Doe Number Two, and the latest discovery, John Doe Number Three.

Patterns jumped out at the investigators. The crime scenes shared similar terrain and vegetation. The Northport locales where John Doe Two and Three were found separately were eerily alike. Both were at a curve in the road, hemmed in by a dense belt of roadside vegetation that formed a thick screen about fifteen feet deep, beyond which they opened up into a wider, more open area under a canopy of trees, an open space with room to walk around in. In both cases, the curve in the road and the canopies were virtually identical.

In drug-related homicides, of which there was no local shortage, the victims were usually just dumped off the interstate. Here, though, the killer had taken pains to find a remote area where he was unlikely to be interrupted and the bodies were less likely to be found.

The modus operandi (m/o) was the same, as was the way the bodies were displayed. What it added up to was that the murders had been committed by a single individual. His familiarity with the backroads area and the pains he took to hide his crimes indicated that he lived somewhere in the immediate area, within thirty or forty miles of Northport. Police were now faced with a Hog Trail killer, knowing that if he was not stopped, he'd kill again.

South of Punta Gorda, in a remote spot off Highway 41, about a quarter of a mile down Royal Road, lay a trailer camp with about a half dozen trailers. At the rear of the camp stood the trailer of Robert "Bobby" Whittaker, thirty-five, manager of a Wendy's fast-food restaurant. Stocky, with black curly hair and a mustache, Whittaker often played host to a loose-knit group of younger men, most in their early twenties, devotees of the Dungeons and Dragons fantasy role-playing game. Officiating as the Dungeonmaster, Whittaker ran a lot of games out of his trailer. There were always a lot of young guys hanging out there and drinking beer.

On the afternoon of April 16, 1996, hanging out in the trailer, were Whittaker, two guys named Tommy and Zack, and two twenty-one-year-olds, Gary Mastin and Richard "Richie" Montgomery. A high school dropout who couldn't hold a steady job, good-natured, easygoing, and attractive, Montgomery liked beer and money and, according to friends, would do "pretty much anything" to get them, so long as it didn't entail any hard work. For a while, he'd lived in Whittaker's trailer as his roommate, but it hadn't worked out. He now lived with his sister, Carla, in another trailer in the same camp.

Today, Richard Montgomery had a secret, but he couldn't keep it all to himself. He told the others that he was going to get a hundred dollars for a couple of hours' work. Whittaker asked if it was legal. Montgomery smirked, saying sarcastically that if it wasn't legal, he'd tell him. He left about fifteen minutes later.

At about 4:30 P.M., he was seen walking along Taylor Road (off Royal), by his brother-in-law, Jeff Whisenant, and the latter's buddy, Ray, who were driving by. Montgomery, dressed in a sleeveless shirt and shorts, was walking in the direction of nearby Cox's Lumber yard. Ray honked the horn. Montgomery waved, and kept on walking.

With the Hog Trail area being used as a staging ground for serial murder, mutilation, and who-knew-what else, it was easy to forget that there were still those who used it to hunt hogs. On April 17, 1996, Thomas Edward Reese and Michael Tisch, veteran Charlotte County surveyors, were doing road evaluations off Highway 41, in the north Port Charlotte woods around Willow Street and Trembley Avenue.

Reese was a hog hunter. When the two men were on break, they went back into the brush to move some hog traps. They drove their county pickup truck in fifty to seventy-five yards along a paved road which ran through dense woods. At the end of the paved areas were sites used as dumping grounds, heaped with garbage and trash. It took about five minutes to get back there.

While poking around, they made a discovery: a human head. It lay on a path, on the ground, about fifty feet away. The two men didn't get any closer. They left, notifying police.

The first law enforcement official on the scene was police officer Sergeant Mark Bala. He noted that there were no homes or businesses near the remote, heavily wooded area. He left his car and met surveyor Reese. They walked back, across a stream and through a break in the brush to an open area under a canopy of trees. Reese pointed to the head. Bala didn't touch anything. He set up a perimeter, securing the scene.

The Major Crimes Unit took over. Detective Rick Hobbs, lead investigator on the case, arrived at 1:15 P.M. Sergeant Bala was already there and about five other Charlotte County and Northport Police Department investigators. They went back in the woods 300 to 400 feet, to the creek. They saw a human skull, then a pelvis. Hobbs was the first to spy a sheet of carpet foam padding, from beneath which protruded a human arm. At that moment, the searchers were unsure whether it belonged to a dead body or a live transient sleeping underneath it.

Hobbs lifted the carpet, exposing the dead body of a young, white, adult male. But not the body belonging to the severed head. This was a second corpse, complete with head, fully intact except for the genitals, which had been removed.

Charlotte County Sheriff's Office Deputy Sheriff Michael Gandy, head of the Major Crimes Unit, stood beside Hobbs as he touched the body, checking for a pulse finding none. No one else touched or tampered with the body. Hobbs laid the carpet padding back down.

The factor of possible contamination of the evidence would later emerge as a key element of the trial. The perimeter was secured, inviolate. No one tampered with the scene.

Todd Terrill of the K-9 Unit conducted a search with his partner, Houston. The dog was trained to detect human-specific enzymes and proteins, invisible but not undetectable to the dog's keen sense of smell. Terrill and Houston surveyed the area. Houston showed interest in a sable palm, eight to ten feet high. One side of the tree appeared flattened. Had one or both victims been tied to the tree?

The murder site was in Charlotte County, but close to the Sarasota County line. Sarasota County Sheriff's Office criminalists arrived, including Lieutenant Bruce Whitehead, senior officer and supervisor, and Nancy Ludwigsen, forensic chemist. Ludwigsen was there to assist in collecting items, such as the skull and other body parts and the carpet foam padding. She put the skull into a pillow case for transportation to the lab.

She also collected hair and fiber samples, an exacting process requiring that she first don a clean gown, gloves, all-new protective gear, and use sterilized equipment. She made a visual inspection of the body, then examined it under ultraviolet light, to ensure that there would be no contamination by the evidence collector. The general areas of the body underwent combings, with the debris separated into envelopes. Each envelope was then labeled according to which area of the body evidence had been taken from.

The crime scene was about three hundred yards away from a cul-de-sac at the end of the paved area. Near that entrance, on a trash pile, Ludwigsen recovered a length of rope as the possible murder weapon.

The head belonged to John Doe Number Four, the body under the carpet padding was John Doe Number Five. John Doe Five had a name: Richard Montgomery. Montgomery had never returned from his clandestine rendezvous of the previous day. John Doe Four was later identified as Kenny Lee Smith, a young, homeless drifter who'd also gone missing.

On April 18, 1996, at St. Joseph's Hospital, an autopsy was performed on Richard Montgomery by Charlotte County Medical Examiner Dr. R. H. Imami, who had also briefly examined the corpse at the crime scene. He began by noting that the subject, Montgomery, twenty-one, an adult male Caucasian, was 5'10" and weighed 138 pounds, with a normal build and flat abdomen. On his neck were two grooves, each a quarter-inch deep, ligature marks made by rope or a similar material.

There were abraded grooves on both wrists, similar to the type of ligature on the neck. A groove mark produced by a rope showed on Montgomery's right lower chest area, while two grooves, an inch apart, marked his abdomen. These rope marks proved that Montgomery had been tied. They were postmortem, having been made after death. The back and buttocks had crisscross abrasions, possibly caused by rubbing against the tree to which the victim had been bound.

The most likely scenario was that Montgomery had been tied to a tree and strangled to death, causing his dead weight to sag against the bonds and inflict the marks after death.

The genitals were missing, excised completely. The cutting had been done with a sharp knife, a fairly precise amputation. There was a minimal amount of blood, indicating that mutilation had been done postmortem.

The anus was dilated more than normal (one inch), possibly indicating penetration by a penis or an object. But there was no signs of trauma or sexual assault, no traces of semen or body fluids, making it impossible to determine if Montgomery had been sexually violated.

The condition of the lung area was consistent with a finding that the subject had died of asphyxia caused by strangulation cutting off the flow of air.

* * *

The grisly double discovery led to the formation of a task force assigned to the case, made up of elements from the state attorney's office, the Florida Department of Law Enforcement, Charlotte County Sheriff's Office, Northport Police Department, and Fort Myers Police Department, about forty investigators in all. The team meshed from the start, working smoothly with good cooperation.

The killer's luck had taken a turn for the worse with the early discovery of Montgomery, his latest kill. Vital clues, some extremely delicate in nature (i.e., microfibers) that would have been lost within a few days' exposure to animals, insects, and the elements, were instead bagged and tagged to become key pieces of evidence.

Autopsy evidence indicated that the victims came from the margins of society. Detective Choiniere told *Court TV,* "The key clue in the victims was the condition of their teeth. Drifters and transients tend to let their teeth go and not receive proper dental care and maintenance, as the average Joe does. John Doe Two (whose teeth were mostly missing), his front teeth were in decent shape. He had fillings missing, abscesses in his back teeth that others would have taken care of, but he didn't. John Doe Three's teeth were in poor condition, almost loose. There was a tooth missing; another pierced through the center by a tooth decay hole. That led us to believe that he had some severe dental problems and for whatever reason he didn't have the means to have them taken care of. So that led us in the direction of looking at transient-type people, soup kitchens, YMCAs, etc."

That made sense from the killer's point of view. He cunningly targeted those who'd sidestepped society's safety net or fallen through the holes—transients, drifters, down-and-outers. Certainly they'd be a lot less likely to be missed than those surrounded by coworkers, friends, and family.

Within two weeks of its start, the task force put undercover agents posing as homeless men on the street. They soon learned that someone had been propositioning transients for nude, bondage-photo sessions in the woods.

This helped clear up the killer's m/o since, except for John Doe Three, there was minimal violence committed on the bodies, apart from the stranglings. Somehow, the killer had been able to win his victims' confidence. This explained how he was able to get them tied to the tree without violence: he was propositioning them to pose for nude bondage photos in the woods. Noted Detective Hobbs, "The killer gains the victim's confidence, there's no real signs of struggle. . . . The victim is already bound, so no special strength is needed."

The case had reached critical mass. The story had gone public. Among those it reached was

Florida's Moore Haven Correctional Institute inmate David Payton, still doing time for grand theft auto. On or about May 8, 1996, Payton told his cell block supervisor that he had information on the Hog Trail Murders. The task force sent a couple of investigators down to interview him.

Payton told them of the events of March 5, 1995, when the driver of a blue Mercury Capri had accosted him outside a Fort Myers park. "I was sitting on a bench when I heard a guy holler, 'Hey!' I went over to the car."

Payton got in, they drove around, Payton getting high on beer, Valium, and marijuana. "When we get to a dirt road, he asked if I'd had my picture taken. I said, yeah. He said, I'll give you money to get your picture taken. . . . He says, I want to tie you up real real tight but I'll let you go. . . . I wanted to go back to Fort Myers."

The car had gotten stuck, the driver got out to join the two helpful hog hunters in freeing it, and Payton found the rope and the knife. "I made up my mind when the car gets out of the ditch, I'm gone. I believe the guy was a psycho and I wouldn't be here if I hadn't stolen that car."

Payton was later released from prison.

The Capri belonged to Daniel Conahan, Sr., an elderly Punta Gorda retiree who said he'd loaned the car to his son on that date. Payton identified that son, Daniel Conahan, Jr., forty-two, as the driver of the blue Capri.

Now the task force had a name, and a suspect, but who was Daniel Conahan, Jr.?

Born May 11, 1954, Conahan was an adoptee. An unmarried, white male, he'd lived in Chicago during most of the 1980s, working as a computer operator for an HMO. In early 1993, he'd come to Florida, moving into his parents' condo in Punta Gorda Isles at Bal Harbor Place, doing the cooking and cleaning for them. In April 1993, he attended a Charlotte vocational tech school, taking a three-month class to become a certified nursing assistant. For a time he worked as private nurse for a quadriplegic. From mid-February through December 1994, he began taking an LPN nursing course.

That was intriguing because the psychological profile of the Hog Trail Killer indicated a middle-aged, white male, high school graduate, maybe some college, living at home. A professional person, possibly a nurse.

Conahan worked briefly as a nurse at the Charlotte Regional Medical Center in Punta Gorda. After three months, he claimed that around January 15, 1996, he'd injured his back lifting a patient. That was the last time he worked at a regular job. He filed for disability and started receiving workman's compensation.

The record showed that Conahan had had few run-ins with the law, but the ones he'd had were significant. In 1978, he'd been discharged from the navy under threat of court martial on several counts of sodomy and physical assault. He was accused of attempting to lure servicemen away from the Naval Training Center, Great Lakes, Illinois, to perform sex acts, and of striking one sailor on the head with a rock when he had rejected Conahan's advances. He denied the charges and was never prosecuted for them. He was also arrested in Chicago in 1980 for soliciting an undercover police officer for illicit sex acts.

Task force members talked to two homeless men who claimed that Conahan had propositioned them and driven to the woods for nude photo sessions. If he couldn't talk them into being tied to a tree, he paid them and dropped them off where he'd picked them up by the roadside.

Choiniere told *Court TV,* "The method of operation in this case is that the perp wanted to find people who were down on their luck, needed quick cash, and could be easily swayed into doing pretty much whatever he wanted. Probably limited education and willing to take a chance. I don't know if all of them were alcoholics or if part of his inducing them was alcohol or drug related. But it's a good possibility that, after a few beers and a few bucks, some of these guys were so much down on their luck that they could be talked into some things that the average person obviously couldn't be.

"If he could not talk them into being tied to a tree, they went back. They were dropped off where he picked them up on the side of the road and no harm done and with probably a couple of bucks in their pocket. People he could tie to a tree obviously didn't come home."

On May 13, 1996, the task force placed prime suspect Daniel Conahan, Jr., under an intense round-the-clock surveillance, which would continue for over fifty days. This was a major effort. The Hog Trail Killer had already slain at least five. He liked to kill and would kill again. If Conahan was the killer, he had to be stopped before he could make his next strike.

Fifteen to twenty members of the forty-plus multicounty task force were assigned to the stake-out. They covered Conahan, his residence, and the two family cars: his father's blue Mercury Capri and his own gray Plymouth Reliant station wagon. Video cameras watched the Punta Gorda Isles Bal Harbor condo from various sightlines, both straight on and through windows and alleys to provide complete coverage. Mobile tracking devices, locator "bugs," were attached to the two vehicles. When Conahan went out of the house, the task force surveillants had an array of vehicles available for shadowing purposes, including unmarked cars, rental cars, pickup trucks. Also on call were a helicopter and a fixed-wing surveil-

lance aircraft, ready to take to the air to follow
Conahan from above.

It didn't take long for Conahan to display pe-
culiar patterns of behavior. He had no job, so he
didn't have to go to work each day. Workmen's
comp for his job-related bad back disability paid
his bills. His daily routine was simple. He'd get
up at mid-morning, going out of the house at
about noon to buy some cigarettes. Then he'd
get into his car and go cruising.

When he'd leave the house, the trackers would
get in their vehicles and follow, also alerting the
aircraft and getting it airborne as a backup. If
they lost the vehicle, the plane or copter would
still be covering it. Conahan was a possible serial
killer. Failure to keep him in view might cause
the death of another innocent victim.

Early in the surveillance, Conahan's behavior
worried investigators, who thought that it meant
they'd been "burned"—discovered. Beginning
his cruising day (often on Highway 41), Conahan
would soon initiate a series of evasive driving ma-
neuvers, as if wanting to elude any possible tail.
He would suddenly drive over the median, jump-
ing it, doing a U-turn and heading away in the
opposite direction. He'd pull into a parking lot,
drive into a space, then leave, continuing on his
way.

Putting their heads together, the trackers rea-
soned that they hadn't been burned, and that this
was Conahan's way of trying to evade any insurance investigators who might have been scrutiniz-

ing him to see if his disability complaint was a real one or bogus. As it later turned out, that was the case. Conahan maintained that he'd been unaware of the surveillance.

Having made these evasive moves, Conahan would then fall back into cruising rhythm, ranging from Port Charlotte to Fort Myers and back again. He went where the transients were, making the circuit of parks, beaches, soup kitchens, and Fort Myers Salvation Army missions. He'd go to the beach and strike up conversations with other men. He'd hang out in the park in Port Charlotte for a while, talk to some people, then move on, eventually returning home.

His mother was in a nursing home and he visited her quite a bit, spending a good deal of time talking to her. Apart from that, he spent most of his time cruising for victims. Florida Department of Law Enforcement Special Agent and task force member Wayne Porter, assigned to the case, commented, "It's not unusual for serial killers to put hundreds of thousands of miles on their vehicles because they are cruising."

The initial surveillance confirmed to police that they were on the right track. Conahan's "whole behavior, his antics while he was cruising, confirmed what we were very suspicious of," Porter said.

Beyond the surveillance, the task force took a more proactive approach with the use of decoys, undercover cops posing as rootless young drifters. One such was Charlotte County Sheriff's Office

Deputy Sheriff Ray Weir, a narcotics officer selected for the assignment because he conformed
to the physical type to which the killer was attracted: young, slim, tanned.

As Conahan traveled back and forth to his
mother's nursing home on Highway 41 between
Fort Myers and Punta Gorda, Officer Weir posed
as a vagrant on that roadway. He dressed for the
role in a sleeveless shirt, torn shorts, old boots,
no socks. On May 17, 1996, Weir stood on the
concrete median at King's Highway and 41, holding a crudely hand-painted cardboard sign saying:
WILL WORK FOR FOOD. He was under surveillance,
but wore no wire.

He was put where Conahan would see him and
could do something about it, whatever that might
be. Conahan's gray Plymouth Reliant station
wagon with tinted windows came over the bridge
from Punta Gorda, driving normally through traffic. He saw Weir from two lanes over and changed
lanes, circled the median and came around for
another pass. Backup officers monitoring the
scene were reminded of a shark circling a victim.

Stopping for the red light, Conahan gave a dollar bill to Weir and asked him if he did any work.
Weir said he'd fallen off a ladder and he had a
bad back, but if it wasn't too hard, he might be
interested.

The next day, May 18, Weir was again in place
on the roadway's concrete median, this time wearing a wireless transmitter, and again under physi-

cal surveillance. Conahan was also covered by a nearby tail car.

Conahan made contact in the afternoon. Driving up in the same vehicle, he stopped for the red light. He gave Weir two quarters and five dimes, asking him if he did any modeling. The light turned green. Conahan went around the block and came back again, resuming the conversation. He propositioned Weir, asking if he was interested in doing a nude photo shoot for a progressive bondage scene.

Weir answered inconclusively and Conahan drove on, but now the task force had him on tape propositioning Weir for a "nude, progressive bondage scene," which is how they theorized the Hog Trail Killer had lured his hard-luck victims into the woods.

On May 23, 1996, at 3:30 P.M., Charlotte County Sheriff's Office Deputy Sheriff Scott Clemens, a Vice Squad detective working undercover, entered Port Charlotte's Kiwanis park. Posing as a homeless transient and wearing a hidden transmitter, Clemens was on assignment to try to make contact with Conahan. As he exited a public bathroom, Conahan approached him, asking, "What's up?"

They left the bathroom together, walking down a park trail. The task force had the woods covered. The trail was wired for audio and video. Planted in the brush, dug into nearby foxholes, were members of the Charlotte County SWAT team, sharpshooters who were poised to fire if Conahan should suddenly attack the undercover officer. Conahan was an unknown quantity, a suspected serial killer. No one knew if he might be armed with a gun, knife, or even a dirty hypodermic needle. They all knew death could happen in a split second.

Conahan asked the other's name. Clemens said his name was Steve. Conahan replied that his name was Steve, too, and asked if he was a police officer. Clemens said, "Absolutely not." Conahan asked if he had hustled. Clemens allowed as to how he might have hustled. Conahan asked if the other would show him his penis for seven dollars. Clemens acted kind of shy, and noncommittal. Conahan asked if Clemens would let him suck his penis for twenty dollars. He said he could go later to an ATM and get the money. Clemens said he wanted the money up front. The subject was more or less dropped. They walked to Conahan's vehicle. Conahan gave Clemens his phone number, saying that he might be back.

The next day, Friday, May 24, dressed in a tank top and shorts, Clemens returned to the park. Conahan walked up and sat down beside him on a park bench. Conahan asked Clemens if he'd done any modeling. Clemens said he had, in high school. Conahan offered him $150 to do some nude photos in a "private area" in the woods. Nude photos taken with a Polaroid.

Conahan asked him how big his penis was and

asked him to show it to him for five dollars. The price was going down. Clemens declined. He walked Conahan back to his vehicle, Conahan importuning him one more time to show him his penis. Clemens said he'd think about it. Conahan drove away.

Clemens told *Court TV,* "He wanted to take pictures of me naked and do some bondage scenes and that's when I started thinking wow, this is the guy."

Security was a top concern. Another time during the surveillance, in one of the parks he frequented, Conahan contacted a stranger, arranging to meet him in a secluded spot. Each got into his own vehicle and headed to a lonely rendezvous in the Punta Gorda woods.

Conahan was under surveillance, so the whole encounter was being observed. But there were drawbacks. The tail cars couldn't follow too closely on the remote dirt roads. The trackers didn't want to burn the whole surveillance project, but they couldn't just lie back and let the prime suspect lure a potential victim to a sylvan slaying.

They decided to call the cops. A marked police car drove into the area, accosting Conahan and his newfound companion, explaining that there had been a complaint lodged of possible illegal dumping, and could they explain themselves and what they were doing?

Conahan and the other said they were picking up cans to sell for recycling. After a while, both men got into their own separate vehicles and drove away. The hidden watchers wondered what might have happened if they hadn't intervened.

The investigation was proceeding along other fronts. Police learned that on April 16, 1996, Conahan had gone to a Punta Gorda Wal-Mart, where credit card receipts showed he'd bought rope, Polaroid film, pliers, and a utility knife. Later that day, he'd gone south on the highway to a branch of the NationsBank, where he'd used an ATM to withdraw forty dollars from his account. Both the store and bank were in close proximity to Cox Lumber, where Richard Montgomery had gone to keep his fatal rendezvous. Conahan had also purchased quarter-inch rope, knives, alcohol, plastic tarps, leather gloves, and Polaroid film at a local store on dates close to the times Kenny Lee Smith and John Doe Two were killed.

The surveillance neared its end as police ratcheted up the pressure another notch. On May 31, 1996, while driving home, Conahan was pulled over by an unmarked task force pickup truck, which herded his car into a Holiday Inn parking lot. He got out of his car. Two plainclothes detectives approached him, saying that he was driving a car similar to one in an investigation they were looking into. They asked if he'd be willing to speak with them. He said he was on his way home. They said it wouldn't take long. They took him into a room in the Holiday Inn which had been turned into a videotape interrogation room. They read him his rights and asked him about the Montgomery case and others they were looking into.

Present at the questioning was Florida Department of Law Enforcement Special Agent Wayne Porter, who introduced himself to Conahan as a "man from the governor's office," and said, "Hi, how you doing?"

Conahan said, "Well, I've been better."

Porter said that the purpose of the interview was either to clear Conahan as a suspect in the Hog Trail Murders, or make him the number-one suspect. Conahan said, "Wow."

In an exclusive *Court TV* interview, Conahan later recalled, "I wanted to help out. And then, as I was being questioned, I realized that, you know, they thought I was the murderer."

They spoke for three hours. It was a game of cat-and-mouse on both sides. Porter felt that Conahan was "cooperating" in order to see how much the police knew. "He was trying to get information from us; he thought he was interviewing us."

Transcripts of the interview show Conahan openly admitted to cruising and engaging in sex with other men, but denied fantasizing about nude male bondage scenes, saying that police would find no material linking him to such "fantasies" at his house. He said, "I have never tied anybody up. . . . It's a fantasy. . . . It's personal, sort of kinky . . . bondage sounds kind of, well, kinky."

At that moment, police were searching the Bal Harbor condo where Conahan lived. Armed with a search warrant, investigators searched Conahan's home and car. Conahan's parents, frail elderly people, were both home when the warrant was served. They were surprised, but not frantically upset, saying that they disbelieved that their son could be involved in anything of that nature.

Police theorized that the blue knapsack they'd seen Conahan carrying back and forth to his car a number of times during the surveillance contained his "murder kit," holding tarps, camera, film, rope, gloves, pliers, and knives. They'd hoped to find this murder kit intact during the search. In his room, they found the knapsack and various items such as clothesline, film, pliers, and a knife, but the items were scattered in various places.

Kenny Lee Smith had been dismembered and forensics had determined that a hacksaw had been used to cut him into pieces. During surveillance, Conahan was photographed coming out of a store carrying a new hacksaw. During the search, the new hacksaw was found in the elder Conahan's toolbox. Daniel Conahan, Sr., denied that it was his, saying that he had an old one and that he didn't know where the new one had come from. Had Conahan used the old one during a crime, gotten rid of it, and replaced it with a new one?

Criminalists swarmed the scene, vacuuming the debris from Conahan's bedroom and furniture and in the two cars. He'd bought knives. Investigators had the receipts to prove it, but where were the knives? Searchers couldn't find them.

For now, though, the police had nothing they could charge Conahan with that a judge wouldn't throw out. They had the credit card receipts, but no witnesses linking Conahan with Montgomery or any of the other victims. They had no DNA evidence linking Conahan to the kills. They had David Payton's testimony, but the statement of a convict currently serving time for stealing Conahan's father's car was hardly definitive. Undercover cops Weir and Clemens had Conahan on tape, propositioning them for nude bondage-photo sessions, but that didn't make him a killer.

Investigators were sure he was the murderer, a serial killer who'd slain at least five and was sure to kill again, but they couldn't prove it. They had to let him go. On May 31, 1996, at the end of the three-hour, videotaped interview, Daniel Conahan, Jr., walked out of the Holiday Inn's impromptu interrogation room a free man.

During a meeting of law enforcement officials involved in the case, a Fort Myers officer recalled that they'd had a similar occurrence in August 1994, where the victim had been tied to a tree and survived a strangulation. Task force investigators went to Fort Myers to examine the file. The two-year-old report, filed among the old cases, made compelling reading.

On August 15, 1994, one Stanley Burden, then twenty-four, had been admitted to a Fort Myers hospital's emergency Room, complaining that a man named "Dan" had tried to kill him. Earlier, Dan had solicited Burden for nude bondage pictures, taken him into the woods, tied him to a tree, and tried to strangle him. Burden furnished a generic description of the attacker and his vehicle.

Since that time, Burden, a transient, had returned to his native Ohio, where he was currently incarcerated in Marion County for child molestation. Charlotte County Sheriff's Office Detective Tom Choiniere and Sarasota County Detective Columbia flew up to interview him. Choiniere recalled, "We try not to get shocked or too surprised, but when Stanley Burden walked out of the lockup area into the interview room with his shirt open, I could see a double ligature scar mark around his neck, which is exactly the same as several of our victims had. And I saw that on his neck and I said, 'Wow, we're in the right spot.' "

Born March 18, 1970, Stanley Burden was 5'10," 142 pounds, with blond hair, blue eyes, and slim, flat-bellied. He'd left Ohio in August 1994, to go to Florida with a companion, staying at a hotel. Not long after arriving, he'd broken a bone in his foot, leaving him unable to work.

The first time he'd met "Dan," Burden had been exiting the men's room at Fort Myers's Lions Park, an area known to be a hangout for male prostitutes. He'd been going out as Dan had been coming in. Later, while Burden was standing in front of a Checkers convenience store, the man had driven up in a gray or silver 1984 car, pulling up in the middle of the road, standing, and calling Burden over to the car. Burden got in, they drove away. The man solicited him to make nude pictures. Burden needed the money. They passed a trucking company. The car pulled off onto a rocky dirt road. Dan offered Burden twenty dollars to let him perform oral sex on him. They got out in a dump area—remote, grassy, screened by trees. Dan pulled a duffel bag out of his car, and they went into the woods. He laid a tarp on the ground. Burden stood on it, peeling off his clothes while the other snapped Polaroid pictures.

Dan used a set of clipperlike pliers to cut lengths of rope, saying he would just drape them over Burden's limbs, to give the illusion of bondage and make the pictures look good. Burden stood against the tree while the other tied him. He then performed oral sex on Burden.

He held Burden's hips, trying to move him into position so he could penetrate him for anal sex. When Burden resisted, Dan got angry. He pulled back the rope around Burden's neck, trying to strangle him. What followed might have seemed grotesquely comic if it hadn't been a matter of life and death.

Dan tried to strangle Burden with the rope. Burden kept turning his head and neck to one side, avoiding having the ropes cut into his windpipe. The other kept tugging at the ropes while Burden kept sliding around the tree. Burden said, "He was tugging for a good half hour. Then he gave up." But it had been a close one, with Burden coming near to blacking out several times before Dan had had enough.

Incredibly, the bantamweight Burden had outlasted the burly would-be killer, exhausting him. Investigators later theorized that Dan had quit because his hands got sore from pulling on the rope. After that, according to credit card receipts, work gloves became part of his murder kit—work gloves and knives.

While Dan prepared to exit, Burden got his foot on the pliers, which the other had used to cut the ropes and carelessly dropped near him. Burden took hold of the pliers and started cutting himself loose.

Dan may or may not have known Burden had the pliers, but suddenly he was in a hurry to leave, gathering up all his things. He offered Burden one hundred dollars to keep quiet. Burden told him to go away and leave him alone. Dan threw his stuff in the vehicle and drove away. Burden cut himself loose and got to the emergency room, where Fort Myers police took his report.

Now, presented with a photo "lineup" of different Hog Trail Murders suspects, Burden picked out Daniel Conahan, Jr., as his attacker.

Highly important was the fact that the incident had been reported back in August 1994, long before Conahan had been tagged as a suspect. The ligature marks on Burden's neck were the clincher. It hardened Burden's testimony against any future defense claims that he'd read newspaper details of the case and cooked up a story about his involvement with Conahan in an attempt to curry favor with the authorities, or to enjoy an ego-boosting turn in the spotlight as a key witness in a big case. As a convicted child molester doing a ten- to twenty-five-year rap, he already had a credibility problem.

The law couldn't yet tie any of the Hog Trail Murders to Conahan, but now they had something concrete they could charge him with and hold him for: the attack on Burden.

On July 3, 1996, the task force made its move, arresting Daniel Conahan, Jr., at his parents' condo. Detective Rick Hobbs was the arresting officer. Conahan was held without bail in Lee County Jail located in the Fort Myers area, on one count each of attempted first-degree murder and kidnapping, and two counts of sexual battery against Stanley Burden.

Neighbors recalled the senior Conahan as keeping to himself, tending his ill wife. The younger Conahan was absent most of the time, they said. During the May 31 condo search, they'd thought police were looking for drugs. Nobody would ever have thought that Conahan would be arrested as a suspected serial killer.

Florida Department of Law Enforcement's Wayne Porter remarked about serial killers, "These are the same kind of people that live next door to you. You think they couldn't participate in such a heinous crime, but that's what they're thinking about every day when you see them come out of their car and go up to their house. They're thinking about the next kill."

Conahan told *Court TV* that he'd been shocked when he'd first learned that investigators suspected him in the Hog Trail Murders, and that later, "When I was arrested, I was again shocked, because I knew I was innocent. And I felt that, how could they arrest me for something like that?"

While he was in jail, one of his two cellmates was John Neuman, held on murder and marijuana charges. Neuman was helpful, showing Conahan how to use the jail's law library, file legal documents and the like.

Conahan was held without bail for seven months on the Stanley Burden charges. In February 1997, a grand jury voted to indict him for the murder of Richard Montgomery. Conahan was moved to the Charlotte County Jail. While there, he remained in contact with Neuman. Meanwhile, Neuman contacted the task force, saying that he wanted to communicate some information about Conahan.

Neuman told investigators that Conahan had said that Richard Montgomery was "his mistake."

THE TRIAL

Three years after his initial arrest on the Burden charges, Daniel Conahan, Jr., would be brought to trial for the first-degree murder, sexual battery and kidnapping of Richard Montgomery in August 1996. Chief prosecutor was Assistant State Attorney Bob Lee, seconded by Jerry Brock. For the defense, attorneys Mark Ahlbrand and Paul Sullivan represented Conahan, who pled innocent to the charges, claiming he'd never even met Montgomery. Ahlbrand said that Conahan might take the stand to testify in his own defense.

As the trial neared, true-crime website APBNews.com's Kevin Heldman ran an interview, dated June 28, 1999, which found Conahan, now forty-five, on antidepressant medicine. Conahan was firing off letters to lawyers, the news media, and the Florida bar, railing that he was being railroaded, and demanding of the authorities, "Where's the evidence?" Conahan said, "If I'm supposed to be tying these guys up, butchering them, cutting their dicks off, wouldn't there be one speck of blood?"

Another time, a handwritten statement from Conahan to APB said, "This is not a case of a serial killer, but a corrupt criminal justice system . . . the police and State Attorney are big on talk but short on proof."

Citing adverse pretrial publicity, Conahan's lawyers succeeded in having the trial moved to nearby Collier County. The trial began on Monday, August 9, 1999, at Collier County Courthouse, 20TH Judicial Circuit Chief Judge William Blackwell presiding. It was a capital murder case, with the state seeking the death penalty.

Around the start of the trial, another body was found in the Hog Trail area. Conahan was a suspected serial killer, but he was being tried for Montgomery only, not the other Hog Trail victims. That material would be excluded from the trial, except on some narrow window rulings.

At the start of the trial, Conahan waived his right to a jury trial, putting his fate solely in Judge Blackwell's hands—a bench trial. Defense counsel Ahlbrand later told reporters that he'd been worried that potential jurors would lie about their exposure to the case and potential bias. As a jurist from neighboring Collier County, outside the perimeter of the Hog Trail Murders, Blackwell's exposure to the case had been minimal, and he was less likely to be influenced by it.

The downside of such a bench trial was that instead of twelve jurors, it only took one person, the judge, to decide Conahan's fate.

Going in, the prosecution had Conahan's receipts for knives, gloves, rope, etc., on or near the same date as Montgomery's death, an ATM withdrawal that same day for forty, not the hundred dollars promised to Montgomery, and fiber micro-evidence. The witnesses: Hal Linde, Conahan's onetime lover, would testify that Conahan had told him of lethal gay bondage fantasies; Bobby Whittaker would put Conahan and Montgomery together, a vital linkage; convict John Neuman would relate the defendant's remarks about Montgomery; and Mary West, Montgomery's mother, would testify as to remarks Montgomery had allegedly made about Conahan. Most of all, though, they had the Man Who Got Away—Stanley Burden.

Assistant State Attorney Bob Lee opened for the prosecution by arguing that Daniel Conahan, Jr., had used the empty promise of easy money to lure Richard Montgomery into rape, death, and mutilation. Conahan promised to pay one hundred dollars to Montgomery for some nude-bondage modeling. Once he was in the woods, bound to a tree and helpless, Conahan raped him, strangled him to death, and cut off his genitals.

Why? Sex. This was the defendant's turn-on. Conahan's dark fantasy was to pick up a hitchhiker, tie him to a tree, rape, and kill him. Montgomery was gullible, a high school dropout, drug and alcohol abuser, who'd do foolish things when he wanted drink or money.

On April 16, 1996, Conahan had gone to a Wal-Mart, buying rope, Polaroid film, pliers, and a sharp-bladed utility knife. He then withdrew forty dollars from a nearby ATM—"show money," according to Lee, bait that he would flash to lure his victim. He picked up Montgomery at Cox Lumber and drove along the trails into the woods. Using the pretext of a "nude progressive bondage" photo shoot, he persuaded Montgomery to allow himself to be bound by rope to a tree. Once secured in restraints, Montgomery was sexually assaulted and then a length of rope was used to strangle him to death. Conahan mutilated the body, using the knife to remove Montgomery's genitals with surgical precision, to prevent the DNA from his saliva from being recovered from them.

"His terrible lust and passion spent and his dark fantasy fulfilled, he walked away with his gruesome trophy in hand," Lee said.

The defense's Ahlbrand conceded that Montgomery had "an interest in casual sex with men, but he's never pushy about it." Conahan didn't dispute that he cruised for casual anonymous sex with male prostitutes. He conceded that he'd spoken of bondage fantasies to detectives interviewing him at the Holiday Inn session. But that didn't make him a killer. The defense argued that Conahan was being persecuted for his lifestyle, that he was being railroaded by a smalltown police force desperate to find someone on whom to hang the Hog Trail killings. The prosecution had no murder weapons and no DNA linking Conahan to Montgomery. Conahan's back problems precluded him from committing the "brutal, physically demanding" crimes. No witness except Bobby Whittaker could even put Conahan together with Montgomery, and he was mistaken or lying. To prove it, the defense had subpoenaed Carla Montgomery, the victim's sister, to testify for the defense.

Opening arguments ended before noon, court going into recess until the next day.

On Tuesday, 9:00 A.M., the parade of prosecution witnesses began. First up were Thomas Reese and Michael Tisch, the two Charlotte County surveyors whose discovery in the woods had led police to the remains of John Does Four and Five. What they'd discovered was a human head, the skull of John Doe Four, Kenny Lee Smith. But Conahan was on trial not for the murder of Kenny Smith, but that of Richard Montgomery. Testimony relating to the other deaths was largely inadmissable. The defense fought to keep as much of it out of the trial as they could. The questioning of the two witnesses skirted the subject, with the prosecutor asking them if they'd seen something "suspicious" in the woods, and how they alerted police to the discovery. The "suspicious object" was, of course, Kenny Smith's skull, but that wasn't allowed into the record.

Charlotte County Deputy Sheriff Michael Gandy, in charge of the Major Crimes Unit at the scene on April 17, 1996, told how lead detective Rick

Hobbs had first seen the sheet of carpet padding and lifted it, unveiling Montgomery's body. He said that he stood beside Hobbs when he lifted back the carpet, that Hobbs had checked for a pulse, and that after determining the man was dead, had laid the carpet back down. The perimeter was secured, and no one tampered with the scene. The state wanted to establish that there had been no contamination of the micro-evidence.

Sarasota Sheriff's Department Forensic Chemist Nancy Ludwigsen told of collecting evidence at the scene and on Montgomery's body. She said that some 300 yards away from the crime scene and body, near the entrance to the trail, on top of a trash heap, she'd recovered a length of rope, which was taken to the lab.

Dr. R. H. Imami, the Charlotte County Medical Examiner, on April 18, 1996, had performed Montgomery's autopsy. He testified that he had found two grooves on the subject's neck, ligature marks by rope or a ropelike material. There were similar marks on Montgomery's right side lower chest area and a pair of horizontal grooves across the abdomen. The grooves were all the same width, a quarter of an inch. The body also displayed crisscross injuries and abrasions on the back and buttocks.

Lee said, "Are those consistent with injuries sustained with being tied to a post, especially if the body was moved?"

"It could be," Imami said.

"What about the external genitalia?"

"They were missing, excised completely."

"What kind of instrument made that amputation?"

"Any sharp knife." Imami said that it had been done precisely, with a sharp, smooth-edged knife or scalpel—"a precise amputation, very precise."

The questioning now moved to the subject of sexual battery, whether the victim had been sexually violated. Imami noted that the deceased's anus was dilated to a width of one inch, larger than normal, which could indicate a sexual assault.

Lack of heavy bleeding showed that Montgomery's genitals had been removed after death. Imami ruled the official cause of death as asphyxia, which he defined as "the stoppage of respiration going to the lungs. The person dies of asphyxia, strangulation, pressure produced on the neck, windpipe, so completely that air cannot go down."

Imami said that the ligature marks on Montgomery's throat and a pair of abraded grooves on both wrists were consistent with the quarter-inch rope found near the scene by criminalist Nancy Ludwigsen.

Prosecutor Bob Lee tried to establish that the grooves on Montgomery's wrists, found to have been made postmortem, could have been caused by the victim's dead weight pressing on the ropes tying him to a tree or post. The witness said it was possible.

Ahlbrand, on cross-examination, asked if it

wasn't possible that the dilation of the anus could have happened as a result of the muscles relaxing postmortem. Imami agreed it was possible. Ahlbrand asked if he had seen any signs of physical trauma sustained by sexual assault. Imami said he'd found no such signs of trauma in the anal area.

Ahlbrand pressed. "Were tests for the presence of sperm and semen performed on the body?"

"Yes," Imami said. "We found no evidence of biological fluids consistent with a sexual encounter."

On redirect, the prosecution returned to whether or not Montgomery had been sexually assaulted. "If the individual had anal intercourse, a penis in their anus, would you find evidence of trauma?"

Imami said, "You may or may not." He could not say definitively whether or not Montgomery had been raped.

The prosecution next focused on Montgomery's background, his friends and family, the net of associations which they maintained linked him to Conahan. Jeff Whisenant was Richard Montgomery's brother-in-law, having once been married to Montgomery's sister, Carla, from whom he was now divorced. He'd known Montgomery since November 1990.

Lee asked, "What kind of things did he like?"

Whisenant said, "He liked to party, drink beer,

run around with his buddies." Montgomery used drugs, the witness said.

"At the time you knew him, he had difficulty holding a steady job?"

"Yes."

"Let me direct your attention to April 16, 1999. Did you see Richard Montgomery?"

"Yes." At about four-thirty that day, he'd been a passenger in a car that drove past Montgomery, who was walking on Taylor Road toward Cox Lumber. The driver honked the horn. Montgomery waved, and kept on walking.

Ahlbrand, on cross, established that Whisenant and Carla Montgomery moved into the trailer park in 1995, and that Richard Montgomery moved in with them early in 1996, living with them for four to five months. He'd moved in with them because he'd moved out of the trailer in which he'd lived briefly with Bobby Whittaker.

Ahlbrand said, "There were 'personality' problems between Montgomery and Whittaker. Were they caused by sexual tension?

"I don't know," Whisenant said. "The problem was related to Bobby. Richard once told me that Whittaker was starting to mess with him."

"So Richard was living with you and Carla."

"I was trying to help the kid."

"Did you have a pretty good relationship with Bobby?"

"As neighbors. That's it." Whisenant said that Whittaker was already living in the trailer park when he moved in in 1995. There was a lot of traffic around Whittaker's trailer, people coming and going. Whisenant "didn't know who was who. All kinds of people. Young boys, younger than I am, eighteen, twenty-two, twenty-three, twenty-four. There was a lot of traffic going in and out of Whittaker's trailer. I couldn't help but see it."

Had Whisenant called the police to complain about the commotion? "I did once," the witness said.

Gary Mastin, twenty-one, lived on Royal Road near the trailer park. He knew Richard Montgomery from seeing him at Bobby Whittaker's place, and had last seen Montgomery at Whittaker's on the afternoon of Tuesday, April 16, 1996, between the hours of 1 and 4 P.M. Montgomery was asleep in a chair in the trailer for part of the time. When Montgomery got ready to leave, Mastin said, "he said he was going out to make some money and that he'd be back in half an hour."

"Did anyone ask him how he was going to do it?"

"Bobby asked him if it was legal."

"What was Mr. Montgomery's response?"

"If it wasn't legal, he'd tell him. He smiled." Mastin said that Montgomery left about fifteen minutes after making the statement.

Robert "Bobby" Whittaker, 35, of Punta Gorda, said he'd first met Richard Montgomery around January 1994, and that they'd been roommates for a few weeks early in 1996. In April of that year, Montgomery was living with his sister.

Lee said, "What kind of person was he [Montgomery]?"

"He was outgoing and carefree." Whittaker said that Montgomery had a "little bit" of a problem with alcohol.

"How often would he drink alcohol?"

"As often as he could get it from someone," Whittaker said. Montgomery didn't have a car. If he wanted to go somewhere, he'd get a ride from someone he knew, or walk. But he rarely left the neighborhood. He'd do odd jobs for a beer or two.

Lee said, "Do you know Daniel Conahan?"

"Yes."

"Who introduced you to him?"

"Jeff Dingman." That was a number of years ago, two years before he knew Montgomery.

According to the prosecution, Jeffrey Allen Dingman was the link between Conahan and Whittaker, and through Whittaker to Montgomery. Dingman had been living in Whittaker's trailer from April through December 1995. In his deposition, Dingman stated that one night when he'd been hitchhiking, Conahan had picked him up and given him a ride. Conahan invited him to the condo—his parents were away. Conahan plied him with booze and pills. They drove around the back roads, Conahan's backpack in the car. Conahan asked if he could tie Dingman naked to a tree and take photos of him for twenty dollars. Dingman said no. Conahan accepted the rejection without fuss, and he and Dingman maintained friendly relations. Conahan admitted visiting Dingman at Whittaker's trailer a number of times, until Dingman had moved out in December 1995 but denied ever meeting Montgomery at Whittaker's or anywhere else.

Lee said, "Did Daniel Conahan come to the trailer? How many times have you seen him?"

"Three times at most." Whittaker said that two-and-a-half to three months before April 1996, Conahan had come to the trailer, looking for Richard Montgomery. Conahan said that Montgomery's sister, Carla, had told him Richie could be found there. Whittaker didn't think Montgomery was there. He thought he may have been out with his brother-in-law, Jeff Whisenant.

Lee returned to the day that Montgomery disappeared. Whittaker had been working the day shift at Wendy's, where he was a manager, returning home around five. Present at the trailer were Mastin, "Tommy," "Zack," and Montgomery. Montgomery "was supposed to be gone for a couple of hours," Whittaker said. He thought he'd last seen him around seven, seven-thirty.

Lee said, "When he left your house, did he say anything?"

Whittaker said, "Just that he was going to make some money; he'd be back in two hours. I asked him if it was legal."

"What was his response?"

"A smirk. A smile. But he told me he would be safe."

"Did Richard ever return?"

"No."

Mark Ahlbrand pointed out a discrepancy in the timetable in the version of events given by Gary Mastin and Whittaker. Mastin said he thought he remembered Montgomery leaving at about four. That jibed with Whisenant's recollection of seeing Montgomery walking along the roadside at four-thirty. Whittaker's account put Montgomery's leaving the trailer much later than the others. The defense would seek to exploit these contradictions, using them to throw doubt on Whittaker's testimony and credibility.

Ahlbrand established that Whittaker and Dingman had been living together in the midsummer of 1995, until Dingman moved out in December of that year. "As of Christmas, 1995, Dingman's out. Sometime Conahan shows up in 1996, he shows up asking for Ritchie; he told you that Carla sent him over there."

Whittaker said, "He said Carla sent him over. He asked for Richie. I told him Richie isn't here, and he left."

Seeking to cast further doubt on the witness, Ahlbrand brought up the fact that early in the investigation, Whittaker's police officer brother had worn a hidden bugging device while questioning him about the Montgomery case.

Moving on, defense counsel said, "Did Richie play Dungeons and Dragons?"

Whittaker said, "He just liked to watch."

"How long was he living with you before he left?"

"About a month and a half, six weeks."

"You two guys have a falling out?"

Whittaker said they had mutually agreed that Montgomery would move in with his sister.

On Wednesday, day three of the trial, Carol Powell, manager of a Punta Gorda Wal-Mart on Highway 41, identified credit card receipts that showed that on April 16, 1996, Daniel Conahan, Jr., had purchased a package of clothesline, some Polaroid 600 film, pliers, and a utility knife. Joyce Allen, custodian of the customer accounts records at the NationsBank, identified records which showed that on that same date, at the bank's Madrid Boulevard branch, Conahan had made a withdrawal of forty dollars. Also entered into evidence was a photo which the ATM's video camera had made of Conahan at the time of the transaction.

The transactions were significant not only for themselves but because the two locales also put Conahan in the vicinity of Cox Lumber at about the time that Richard Montgomery was last seen.

Convicted killer John Neuman, Conahan's Lee County Jail cell mate for seven months, testified that at first Conahan had said that he hadn't known Montgomery. But later, after they'd gotten to know each other better, he admitted knowing him, saying they'd gone out together on a few beer runs.

Lee said, "Did he make any comment in particular?"

"At one time, he said that Montgomery was his mistake," Neuman said, adding that Conahan said he'd visited Montgomery's trailer several times, and that he knew his sister.

The defense suggested that Neuman's cooperation with the prosecution had enabled him to bargain down a potential first-degree murder charge to a plea of guilty to manslaughter, trading a life sentence for a prison term of twelve years.

A pathetic note was struck by state's witness Hal Linde, Conahan's ex-lover, who was HIV-positive and shaking visibly from the effects of Parkinson's disease. Now residing in California, he'd first met Conahan years ago, in a Chicago bar.

The prosecutor said, "What kind of a relationship did you and he have?"

Linde said, "A gay relationship."

"You had a gay relationship, you lived together. When was that?"

"Nineteen eighty-eight through ninety-two."

"Did he ever discuss with you a sexual fantasy that he had?"

Linde said that Conahan had once told him that his fantasy was "to pick up hitchhikers, tie them to a tree and fuck them."

"No further questions."

Under Mark Ahlbrand's sympathetic cross, Linde said, "It was just a fantasy. They're making a big deal out of this. I don't think he did anything."

"During the time you knew him, did Conahan tie you up, did he tell you he had done that?"

"Not really."

"Were you worried about him acting that out?"

"No."

"It was an intimate relationship?"

"Yes, it was."

On redirect, Linde was asked of Conahan, "Are you still in love with him?"

Linde said, "Yeah."

At the defense table, Conahan brushed away tears, one of the few outward displays of emotion he would show during the trial. A second, more explosive display would be wrung from him during the testimony of the next witness, Mary West, Richard Montgomery's mother.

From Kissimmee, Florida, West was a nurse/medical supervisor at Osceola County Jail. She'd been divorced from her truck driver husband when Richard Montgomery was two years old. She said that as a child Montgomery was emotionally handicapped, that he had a substance-abuse problem with alcohol. "He just was never able to not drink." When her own mother, his grandmother, died on the night of January 6, 1993, Montgomery confided to West that as a child he'd been sexually abused. His work record was poor. Asked about his general attitude toward life, she described him as "happy-go-lucky."

"After Richard had something to drink, was he very trusting?"

She said, "Oh, yeah."

On cross, Ahlbrand had her clarify her son's living arrangements. First, he'd lived with his sister and brother-in-law, then he moved into a separate trailer for a short time, then he lived with Whittaker, then back with Carla.

West said that she'd never met Conahan. Ahlbrand said, "Did your son ever tell you that he had met a man named Danny?"

"He told me that the last time I saw him, March twenty-third, Saturday. . . . He wanted to talk, wanted to tell me about this new friend he had made." The friend had been in the navy, he'd been a nurse and worked at a medical center, he was an older man. She thought the name was Carnahan. She knew people named Carnahan, but Richard Montgomery had corrected her, saying, it's Conahan.

Later on in the same conversation, Richard Montgomery told her that "someone" had offered him $200 to pose nude.

At the defense table, that got a reaction from Conahan, who said loudly, "She's lying," then added, "You're a liar." Attorney Paul Sullivan put a hand on Conahan's shoulder, trying to calm him down.

Asked why she hadn't mentioned this to police, she said she had. The defense pointed out that no record of such a statement could be found in the transcript of her tape-recorded interview by

Detective Hobbs on April 18, 1996, "two days after your son was killed, one day after they found his body. Nowhere in that statement did you ever mention that your son had contact with a 'Mr. Carnahan'."

She countered that it must have been during one of the passages in the transcript marked as "inaudible."

Shifting gears, Ahlbrand asked if her son had told her why he'd moved out of Bobby Whittaker's trailer. She said, "He didn't like the way he stared at him; there was a sexual theme, he felt uncomfortable."

On redirect, Bob Lee inquired further into what Montgomery might have told the witness about Conahan. She said, "I remember him telling me, his new friend worked at the medical center." She admitted that Montgomery had said nothing linking Conahan to nude photos.

She said that she'd tried to warn him. "I told him that a psychopathic personality could lure someone like my son out, someone could do things to him, kill him. I told him all that. He didn't believe me. He said, no one will kill me, no one will kill me, I will kill them first."

Defense implied that Mary West had tailored her account to fit with stories she'd read in the newspapers. She said she hadn't.

Fort Myers Police Department Detective Pedro "Pete" Soto took the stand, telling how on August 15, 1994, he'd gone to a hospital emergency room to interview Stanley Burden, who'd given him a pair of pliers he said belonged to "Dan." (Soto later remarked to *Court TV* that when he'd first seen Burden, the scars on his neck reminded him of that old Clint Eastwood movie, *Hang 'em High,* where the actor plays the survivor of a Wild West lynching.) For the defense, Ahlbrand elicited the information that Soto had felt that Burden was not entirely forthcoming.

On the night of August 15, 1994, emergency room nurse Suzanne Hartwick had been on duty and treated Stanley Burden. She said, "There were abrasions around his neck, scrapes on his back and chest, abrasions around his wrists and on his ankles." She described the marks around his neck as "two rings, two pretty wide abrasions, [reaching] almost to the back."

"Did Burden make any statement how he got the injuries; did he mention who did this? Please tell us how Burden received the injuries."

Hartwick said that Burden had said that approximately fifteen minutes before he'd entered the emergency room, he'd been assaulted by a man named Dan, who'd tried to rape and kill him.

On cross, defense got her to confirm that Burden had entered the emergency room on foot, under his own power, implying that his injuries were not too severe.

* * *

Now came the death-cheater himself, arguably the last person on earth that Daniel Conahan, Jr., wanted to see in that courtroom, Stanley Burden, currently on loan from the DeSoto County, Ohio's, Jail. Neat and clean, with neatly trimmed hair, wearing glasses, dressed in a gray suit and tie, Burden, twenty nine, took the stand.

Lee's direct began by noting Burden's physical description in August 1994, at the time of the attack: tall, slim, blond, flat bellied, and tan, underlining his likeness to Richard Montgomery, a physical type craved by the killer.

Burden told of the car which he'd gotten into on August 15, 1994. "It was gray, silver. It looked like Christmas inside. It was like the dash and everything was dark red, the seating had green and red weaved through it. The windows were tinted." Conahan's car was a gray Plymouth Reliant with tinted windows.

Lee said, "Did he make you an offer?"

Burden said, "He started talking about pictures."

"What kind of pictures?"

"Nude pictures."

Burden said they drove past a trucking company, the driver pulling onto a dirt road, halting at a metal mesh fence beyond which lay a dumping ground, a remote area. Conahan removed a duffle bag from his car, and he and Burden went into the woods. Conahan laid a blue tarp on the ground and told Burden to "take off my shirt, show a little bit of hip." Conahan started taking pictures with his Polaroid.

"While he was taking the pictures, he would say, get into this position and that position. He wanted pictures of me getting erect," Burden said. "He kept taking photos, telling me to take my pants down further."

Conahan told him to step over to the tree. The defendant used a pair of red-handled pliers to cut various lengths of rope. Burden stood with his back to a tree, pants down, while Conahan loosely draped the ropes over him, to "simulate bondage." The ropes binding him to the tree circled his neck, chest, and legs. Burden complained that mosquitoes were biting him. Conahan, standing behind him, yanked on the ropes, pulling them tight.

Lee asked, "Did he touch you?"

Burden said, "Yeah, he was trying to get me while I was tied to the tree."

"Did he commit oral sex?"

"Yes, he was going down on me trying to get me erect."

"Did he attempt other sex?"

"He tried to position me, he had his hands out, he was trying to get me to the side, he was trying to penetrate me."

"I have to ask, with which part of his body?"

"His penis."

"What was it like, as you resisted?"

"I kept trying to put myself in the middle of

the tree. . . . He tried to keep a straight face, but I know he got angry."

"Was he able to penetrate?"

"No, I kept shifting on him."

"What happened then?"

Burden said that Conahan "snapped" the rope around his neck, pulling it tight, trying to strangle him. For better leverage, he put his foot up against the tree and leaned back on the ropes, putting his weight into it. "He was hitting me in the back, asking me, why won't I die?"

Two strands of rope circled Burden's neck, going around him and the tree. He felt himself fading. "He was strangling me, I was starting to go down," he said. But he decided, "I'm not going like this." Struggling, he kept working himself around the tree.

"How long did he try?"

"He was tugging a good half-hour, before he gave up."

"What did you do in order to survive?"

"I kept turning my neck to the side. As long as the rope didn't cut into the larynx, I was able to breathe," Burden said.

Exhausted, worn out, Conahan was the first to abandon the struggle. Conahan had dropped the pliers near the tree. Burden used his foot to pull them to him. Crouching down against the ropes, he was able to reach the pliers and pick them up, using them to cut the ropes. He didn't know if Conahan saw the pliers in his hands, but at that point, Conahan asked him, "You still want this hundred dollars?"

Conahan then left in a hurry. After he left, Burden freed himself and made his way to the hospital. The next day, he accompanied police officers, guiding them first to the trucking company and from there to the site in the woods. Some of the trees bore rope marks, photographs of which were entered into evidence. Burden also identified the red-handled pliers as those which Conahan had used to cut the rope, and which the witness had taken to the hospital and turned over to the police.

Wrapping up, the prosecutor said, "Mr. Burden, do you still have the scars?"

"Yes, two of them."

He was requested to open his collar and show the scars to the court, which he did—an electrifying moment. Lee said, "The individual who did this, do you see him here?"

"Yeah," Burden said, pointing at Conahan.

"He has indicated the defendant," Lee said.

Burden stated that he'd been promised nothing for his testimony—no deals, no monetary rewards, nothing.

The defense's Paul Sullivan argued that Conahan had paid Burden for oral sex at a time before August 15, 1994, when he'd been admitted to the emergency room. "You're in a park that was a hangout for male prostitutes . . . you knew Lion's Park was a place where male prostitutes hang out." When Conahan had pulled up in his car, calling Burden over, why hadn't the witness just walked the other way?

Burden said, "When somebody calls me, I come. I got a complex about just leaving."

Sullivan said, "When Mr. Conahan called you over, you voluntarily got into his car. He kept going, around the block. You agreed to go with him and perform the sex act for twenty dollars."

"I've got to help pay for my share of the bills."

"You were the one who told Conahan where to go."

"He took me to the area."

"This is an area where gay people go to have sex."

"I had no idea," Burden said, "I wasn't down here for a month."

"Conahan gave you twenty dollars."

"What I'm saying, he talked about twenty dollars, but when we pulled into the area, up to the area where the mala luca trees are, he changed his mind. He took a few photos and then it went off into the disaster area."

"Did you ever get completely naked?"

"No, my pants went just below my knees. When everything [the ropes] tightened up, he tied my hands, and took the rest of my clothes off."

Focusing on the discrepancies between what he testified had happened, and what he'd told investigators at the time of the attack, Sullivan said, "Why did you tell those lies to the sheriff's office?"

Judge Blackwell admonished the witness, "You listen to the question."

Sullivan said, "Why did you tell lies?"

Burden said, "Because Gerstner [Detective Timothy Gerstner of the Fort Myers Police Department] told me, I've locked people up for prostitution. They're going to lock me up, I made up a big ol' story."

The defense pointed out that while Burden said he'd received nothing for his testimony, Detective Hobbs had told him that a letter describing his participation in the case would be put into his master file, which would be considered when Burden came up for parole in 2002. Counsel expressed skepticism about Conahan's having offered Burden a hundred dollars after trying and failing to kill him. Burden said that Conahan had been in a hurry, gathering up his "stuff" and the duffel bag. "He was talking, He'd give me a hundred, don't say nothing."

Sullivan was doubtful that Conahan could have worn a quarter-inch groove into the tree with his bare hands while trying to choke Burden. "He's trying to choke you and he gives up?"

Burden said, "Yeah, he was hitting me over the head as he's yanking, he was pulling back. . . . He asked me, why don't I die, make his job easier."

Wasn't it true that Burden had told a reporter that he hadn't told police everything, but held back information, because of, as he put it, "just the badge alone"?

Burden said, "When he [Gerstner] told me he was locking people up for prostitution, I didn't tell them everything."

Sullivan reminded the witness that he'd described himself as a "habitual liar." Burden said that he was cured of lying. "Prison taught me that."

Charlotte County Sheriff's Office Deputy First Class Scott Clemens testified that while working undercover posing as a transient, on May 23, 1996, he'd made contact with Conahan in Kiwanis Park. Clemens was wired with a hidden bug to transmit any conversation.

Meeting Conahan on a trail outside the men's room, Clemens said his name was Steve. Conahan introduced himself as Steve. A tape of Conahan soliciting the officer was admitted into evidence. At one point, Conahan is heard saying, "I'm not going to touch you or anything. I just sort of want to see what you look like nude. Get an idea. Is that all right?"

The following day, they met again, Conahan asking the other if he'd done any modeling. Clemens said he'd done some in high school. Conahan offered him $150 to do some nude photos in a private area.

Clemens said, "He said I would have to do them nude, and I would have to be erect for some of them. . . . He said he needed to know how well endowed I was, I said I was average. He offered me five dollars to show him my penis. I told him I wouldn't do it. He walked back towards his vehicle, got into it. He asked me one more time, if he could see my penis, it would take five minutes.

"I said I would think about it."

Thursday, day four, began with Charlotte County Sheriff's Office Deputy Ray Weir taking the stand to testify about how he'd worked undercover in May 1996, standing out on the median on Highway 41, along a route taken by Conahan. Conahan gave him a dollar and asked him if he was looking for work. Weir said he told him, "I've got a bad back, but if it wasn't too hard, maybe I'd be interested."

On tape, Conahan said: "Yeah, you know, basically it's, uh, it'd be nude modeling. I don't know if you could get into that or not, you know. But I hope you'd think about it. I do have a model lined up for tomorrow, and I'm paying a hundred and fifty. Some of these pictures are on the kinky side, so I don't know if you'd be into it, you know."

Weir said, "Well, more money or something, money talks, you know what I'm saying?"

Conahan went on. "Maybe stripping, different poses nude and then maybe a progressive bondage scene, you know, that I want to do."

* * *

Now came the crime scene investigators, the criminalists, technicians, evidence collectors, lab workers, and analysts. The state contended that a substantial body of micro-evidence linked Conahan to Richard Montgomery's murder. Witnesses testified how the evidence was collected at the crime scene and during the May 31, 1996, search of Conahan's condo and cars, establishing an unbroken chain of possession of uncontaminated evidence. Karen Cooper, a veteran, twenty-year crime lab analyst, had vacuumed sweepings from Conahan's gray Plymouth Reliant, his father's dark blue Mercury Capri, and his bedroom. The Reliant yielded a blue beach towel; the Capri a blue tarp and blue baseball cap.

In each area, a standard vacuum cleaner with a filter was used to collect the sweepings, which were then bagged and sealed. The packages were turned over to the Charlotte County Sheriff's Office.

More witnesses followed, with similar testimony, identifying bags and state exhibits: the towel from Montgomery, debris that came off the sheets used to wrap the different body parts found at the crime scene.

Charlotte County Sheriff's Office Lieutenant Michael Gandy testified that during his May 31, 1996, interview of Conahan, the defendant indicated that he had access to the Mercury Capri, and that he had driven it within a month or a month and a half of that interview.

* * *

An intense, dramatic episode occurred on Friday, day five of the trial, as the murdered man's sister, Carla Montgomery, took the stand to testify—for the defense. Conahan's lawyers had subpoenaed her. The prosecution's next witness was temporarily unavailable, and Carla Montgomery had come in from out of town, so it was agreed to let the defense go out of order and call her to the stand. She was not happy about having to testify on Conahan's behalf. Ahlbrand began by asking her about her brother's living arrangements, focusing on his brief stay with Bobby Whittaker. "Your brother stayed there not for a very long period of time, he then moved back in, correct?"

She said curtly, "Yes."

"Did you appreciate the level of his discomfort? Did you understand it?"

"Yes."

"Would you consider yourself a good friend of Whittaker?"

"No."

Richard Montgomery had been living with her in her trailer right up to the time he was killed, but he'd continued to hang out at Whittaker's trailer.

Whittaker had testified that two months before April 16, 1996, Conahan had appeared at the trailer, looking for Richard Montgomery, saying that Carla Montgomery had steered him there. Now, Carla Montgomery said under oath that she'd never seen Conahan before. Ahlbrand said,

"Do you ever remember anyone coming over to your trailer asking for Richie, and you sending him over there [Whittaker's trailer]?"

"Not that I can remember."

In the afternoon, testimony vital to the state's case was presented by Paula Sauer, a Florida Department of Law Enforcement crime lab micro-analyst. She'd gone through the various evidence, collecting debris and vacuum bags, searching for fibers. Among Montgomery's pubic hair combings, she'd removed a paint chip. She'd examined vacuum sweepings from the Mercury Capri, debris from a coat found at the crime scene, sweepings from Conahan's bedroom floor and furniture, debris from the cap found in the Capri, vacuum sweepings from Conahan's Plymouth Reliant station wagon, and fibers from the rope found near the crime scene.

Court recessed for the weekend, resuming on Monday, August 17, microanalyst Paula Sauer returning to the stand to complete her testimony. Sauer identified sixteen different fiber types, fifteen of which were consistent with fibers found in Conahan's house and cars. The sixteenth fiber type, recovered from Conahan's residence, matched fibers on the rope used in August 1994, to try to strangle Stanley Burden.

The fiber evidence included four or five rare pink polypropylene fibers from the foam padding covering Montgomery's body, three fibers from the towel used to cover Montgomery's face, nine fibers from the sheet which had been used to wrap him, three found in the rope, and two from the body and Mercury Capri debris.

The pink polypropylene fibers were found on Montgomery's body, and a rope found at the crime scene, and the Mercury Capri. Similar purple-brown acetate fibers were found in the foam padding, Conahan's bedroom, and the Capri. Gold and black fibers were found in the foam, the Mercury, the blue cap, and Conahan's bedroom. Other yellow rayon fibers were found in the sheet used to transport Montgomery's pelvis, Conahan's knapsack, the Reliant, the Capri, the blue cap, and Conahan's bedroom. Sauer's professional opinion was that all the fibers could have originated in Conahan's bedroom.

Red nylon carpet fibers were found in the two cars and on the towel investigators had used to cover Montgomery's face. Green acrylic fibers were found on the sheet used to transport the body, the coat found at the scene, the two cars, and Conahan's bedroom.

Sauer said, "All of these fibers are consistent, they share the same source. A large number of fibers were found in Conahan's bedroom; his bedroom is the source."

Green wool fibers found on the rope used on Burden were consistent with those found in the Capri, Sauer said. Fibers found on the remains of Kenny Lee Smith were also linked to Conahan. Prosecution and defense then wrangled on what evidence was admissible. Judge Blackwell refused to allow the Kenny Smith fiber findings into evidence, but let in the fibers found on the rope used in Stanley Burden's attempted murder, ruling it admissible because of the similarities between the attacks on Burden and Montgomery.

Florida Department of Law Enforcement senior crime lab analyst Janice Taylor followed, testifying about her examination of the paint chip gleaned from Montgomery's pubic hair combings. She found that the chip, which had four layers, came from a car which had been repainted twice. It was consistent with the paint job on the dark blue Mercury Capri. The repainted Capri's layers corresponded with those of the paint chip found on the victim.

Taylor said, "These two paint chips were indistinguishable from each other." In tests, the chips even shared the same chemical reactions. Her conclusion: the chip came from a 1984 Mercury Capri or another car with a four-layer paint composition.

The last of its thirty-eight witnesses having testified, the state rested.

Defense moved for an aquittal, arguing that the state had failed to prove first-degree murder, kidnapping, and sexual battery. Ahlbrand argued that there was no proof that Montgomery had been forcibly sodomized, noting that the medical examiner had found the anus dilated, but no signs of tears, trauma, or semen in the cavity. He offered a hypothetical alternative explanation about what had happened, suggesting that Montgomery's death had resulted from a nude progressive bondage scene that got out of hand. "A reasonable hypothesis is that things moved along too quickly and the man died."

The judge dismissed the sexual battery charges, letting the murder and kidnap charges stand.

Tuesday, August 17, the seventh and last day of the trial. Taking the stand was Daniel Conahan, Jr., even though he'd been advised by the court that his failure to testify could not be held against him; Conahan was the enigma at the center of the case. It was tough to get a read on him, his demeanor didn't give away much. During his time in jail, he'd gained weight. He was short haired, clean shaven, round faced, bearish. He seemed like an ordinary citizen, but even defense counsel Mark Ahlbrand had once said of his client to an interviewer, "He's either an innocent man who's going to the chair or the most depraved, sick individual you'll meet."

Conahan gave his version of the meeting with Stanley Burden. He was unable to recall the day, week, or month of the encounter, he said, but he remembered that it happened at about 11:30 A.M., as he was driving his Plymouth Reliant down Highway 41.

He said, "I saw him cross the street that bordered the north part of Lion's Park. He was preparing to cross the street. He put his thumb out and grabbed his crotch."

"When he grabbed his crotch, did you think he was receptive?"

"Yes." Conahan drove back and propositioned Burden, who got in the car. "I offered him twenty dollars to perform oral sex on me and I would perform oral sex on him."

Conahan said he was unfamiliar with Fort Myers roads and that Burden had told him where to drive, guiding him to a semiwooded area off Palmetto Street. "I engaged with oral sex on him; he performed oral sex on me."

When they were done, Conahan drove Burden back to Lion's Park: "He wanted to make some more money."

"Did you mention the prospect of photography, in the context of bondage? You asked him to pose for some pictures?"

"Yes, I did."

"Was he receptive?"

"No," Conahan said, adding that Burden had mentioned that he had a friend who might be interested in posing.

"Did you take Mr. Burden to the woods and try to kill him?"

"No."

Defense counsel next addressed the statement of Jeff Dingman, Bobby Whittaker's ex-roommate, whose deposition told of his first meeting with Conahan, when Conahan had picked him up hitchhiking and propositioned him to pose for nude bondage in the woods.

Conahan stated that he'd indeed seen Dingman as a possible sexual contact when he'd picked him up that night in early 1995. Then he'd learned that Dingman was married and that was one of the reasons why he had not solicited him. From April through December 1995, Conahan had gone to visit Dingman "ten or fifteen times" at Whittaker's trailer. "I didn't care for Mr. Whittaker," Conahan said, adding somewhat fastidiously that he tried to keep a clean house and that he found the slovenly condition of Whittaker's trailer "disgusting."

As for Richard Montgomery, Conahan said that he'd never seen or met him.

On cross, Bob Lee focused on Conahan's movements on April 16, 1996, establishing that Conahan's residence was within a couple of miles of Highway 41, Wal-Mart, the NationsBank, and Cox Lumber. He asked if part of Burden's attraction for Conahan was because he was a street person, a hitchhiker. "Wasn't that part of the attraction? Isn't it true that you had a fantasy about picking up a hitchhiker, tying him to a tree, and having sex with him? Isn't it true it's a fantasy?"

Conahan said, "No, not really . . . I have fantasized about bondage. I did not say picking up a hitchhiker. My fantasy is bondage, but not hitchhiker bondage . . . that's not my only fantasy."

"You do hold and have held a fantasy that involves bondage and includes tying them up in the woods, isn't that true?"

"Yes."

"Thank you," Lee said. "Now in August 1994, at the time you were having this encounter with Stanley Burden, you were having problems physically?"

The defense objected as to the relevance. Lee said it was related because Conahan's physical problems prevented him from strangling Burden, and Judge Blackwell let him continue the line of questioning.

Lee said, "Did you have back problems and a sprained arm?"

Conahan said, "I have had back problems for quite a long time."

"Do you recall going to seek treatment for back spasms on July 20, 1994, less than a month before Burden?"

"I have gone several times for back spasms; I do remember going to the doctor, I don't recall that date."

Lee returned to Whittaker's statement that Conahan had showed up at the trailer about two months before April 16, 1996, seeking Montgomery. "You have been to Whittaker's trailer. . . . Is that the same trailer in which Montgomery lived?"

Conahan said, "I don't remember. That's what I have read in the reports. I have never seen or met Mr. Montgomery."

"Isn't it true that you went to Whittaker's

trailer [looking for Montgomery], that when you were surprised at seeing Whittaker there, you came up with a story that Carla Montgomery sent you there?"

"That is not true!"

Lee pointed out that while Conahan testified that he'd been to the trailer some ten or fifteen times, on May 31, 1966, he'd told investigators that he'd only been there a couple of times. Conahan said that he'd last visited Dingman at the trailer in December 1995, shortly before he'd moved out.

On redirect, the defense addressed Conahan's inconsistencies about how many times he'd visited the trailer as a product of his anxieties during the May 31, 1996, interview. "You knew you were suspected of being involved in a murder. You didn't tell them the truth then, did you?"

Conahan said, "I was very nervous."

"You were being accused of murder."

"Yes."

"In reality, you had been out there as of December 1995."

"Yes."

On reredirect, Lee said, "When counsel said you weren't being honest, you didn't tell them the truth, did you?"

Conahan said, "No."

"And even though they were asking you about a murder, they treated you very nicely. They were cordial."

"They were nice."

At the conclusion of Conahan's testimony, nothing had been revealed. But Florida Department of Law Enforcement Special Agent Porter had no doubts about Conahan, telling *Court TV,* "He's a con [man], he's been a con all his life, conning people that he's a nice guy. . . . When he takes the mask off, you see the true monster that he is."

Handling the state's closing was Bob Lee. "Hal Linde, the defendant's homosexual lover for six years in Chicago, testified that the defendant had a fantasy of picking up hitchhikers, tying them up, and having sex with them. It's clear that Linde still loves Conahan. Conahan's former lover held something back, what he did not say was the ultimate culmination of the fantasy—to not just tie them up, but then murder them. "Burden's neck wounds speak volumes, and the subsequent witnesses prove that this was more than an idea, this was something Conahan was determined to fulfill." Lee cited the testimony of undercover cop Scott Clemens, whose physical profile was not unlike Richard Montgomery's, and who was propositioned by the defendant for nude progressive bondage:

"Through this testimony, we see Conahan's plan and scheme, how he sets the trap to bring about the fantasy. The way in which he went about fulfilling his secret desires is the defendant's signature, the unique identifiable points of similarity, identifying the defendant as the murderer."

Lee noted Conahan's approach to undercover cop Ray Weir, whom he'd offered $150 for nude progressive bondage. The key was the officer's conformity to Conahan's "type": slim physique, down on his luck, a desperate need for money.

He said, "This is part of the defendant's dark sexual fantasy. What makes a person sexually attractive is very relevant. What we see him acting out is homosexual fantasies. His motive to target and single out Richard Montgomery—a fantasy nearly fulfilled with Burden and satisfied with the murder of Richard Montgomery."

Lee cited Mary West's statement that her son had told her about his new friend, Conahan; Bobby Whittaker's account of Conahan's visit to the trailer, looking for Richard Montgomery; John Neuman's quoting Conahan as saying Montgomery was his "mistake"; and Jeff Whisenant's sighting of Montgomery near Cox Lumber. He retraced Conahan's movements on April 16, 1996: driving north from Punta Gorda on Highway 41, stopping at Wal-Mart to buy clothesline, Polaroid film, pliers, and a razor-sharp utility knife.

"We've seen all of these in the attack against Burden. Now the defendant has added a knife, a knife he will use to excise the victim's genitals after he is killed to eliminate DNA evidence," he said. "The knife's addition shows his deadly desire and confirms his premeditation. At six-twelve P.M., driving south toward Cox Lumber, he uses the ATM machine. It's very significant as to what he does there. He doesn't take out two hundred dollars, or one hundred and fifty. He only takes forty dollars. That's just show money, so the victim will believe he has money. The intention is not to take photos, the intention is to kill. Only one person will come out of the woods."

The micro-evidence was weighty, Lee said. "If it was just one or two fibers, or even a dozen, there might be some possibility, we might imagine a secondary transfer to a friend, Dingman to Montgomery, ultimately to that terrible crime scene. But there are hundreds of fibers.

"If it was just the fibers alone, some still might speculate, but not when one considers the multilayered paint chip, not when the physical evidence is combined with the testimony of the other victim, Stanley Burden, and not when we recall Conahan's unfulfilled, uncompleted fantasy."

Lee concluded, "The state would submit there is no reasonable doubt, Richard Montgomery was indeed Daniel Conahan's 'mistake.'"

Closing for the defense, Mark Ahlbrand argued that Conahan had been singled out for prosecution not because of what he'd done but of who he was. "The issue in this case is identity." He pointed out that Conahan had chosen to take the stand, strengthening his credibility.

Addressing the sticky issue of Stanley Burden, Ahlbrand conceded, "Burden clearly was strangled. . . . Conahan took the stand and says he did have a sexual encounter with him. Burden is a psychotic liar and can fool truth-detection devices." Conahan had a sexual encounter with Burden, but not on August 15, 1994, the day Burden was strangled.

Convict John Neuman's testimony could be discounted—he parlayed it into "walking away on a first-degree murder charge." Bobby Whittaker's statement was deceptive. As for Mary West, the implication was that she thought Conahan was guilty of her son's murder and wanted to help convict him.

Ahlbrand said, "We think that Conahan had an encounter with Burden sometime, on a day when Conahan wasn't in school. They had a sexual encounter. Conahan discussed a bondage theme with Burden. We think that Burden was reluctant, Conahan had to leave, and that Burden blended these stories. . . .

"Why did Mr. Burden end up getting strangled?" Ahlbrand suggested that perhaps it had been done by his roommate, and that instead of blaming it on his "sugar daddy," he hung it on Conahan. "Burden had a motive to identify Conahan, he didn't risk the exposure of getting that person involved."

Ahlbrand ridiculed elements of Burden's story: his assailant's inability to strangle a tree-bound victim, the finding of the pliers, Conahan's offering him a hundred dollars to keep quiet as he quickly packs up and exits. "It doesn't wash; there's something more to this story." Burden was up for parole in 2002, he noted.

If Conahan didn't kill Richard Montgomery, who did? Ahlbrand offered a possible suspect: Bobby Whittaker. Montgomery had expressed his uneasiness about living with Whittaker and moved out, but continued to spend a lot of time hanging out at the trailer.

Ahlbrand said, "Is it reasonable to assume that Whittaker gets mixed signals, if he thought that Montgomery was going to reestablish a relationship with him? Is it plausible to think that he might somehow have offended Whittaker?" Were Montgomery's injuries caused by an attempt to remove forensic evidence, or the result of the punishing rage of a "jilted lover?"

On rebuttal, the prosecution's Jerry Brock cited the fiber evidence, with many fibers transferred to the crime scene from Conahan's vehicle, bedroom, personal belongings, and backpack. The paint chip found in Montgomery's pubic hair showed the same four-layer structure as the paint on the blue Mercury Capri. The paint chip tied Conahan to the crime scene and the victim. "That's why he said Montgomery was his one mistake."

He concluded, "Your Honor, based on the totality of the facts and circumstances, we have met our burden of proof."

Judge Blackwell retired to his chambers, emerging less than a half hour later with a decision. Conahan stood as the verdict was read. Blackwell said, "The similarities of the injuries to Burden and Montgomery are established beyond a reasonable doubt. . . . The fibers shared microscopic characteristics." He said that he'd found the testimony of Whittaker, West, and Burden credible.

He delivered the verdict. "Mr. Conahan, it is the judgment of this court that you are guilty of first-degree, premeditated murder of Richard Montgomery and the kidnapping of Richard Montgomery."

Awaiting the death penalty in Florida State Prison, Daniel Conahan, Jr., was interviewed on December 10, 1999, by *Court TV*. Conahan, angry, claimed that the state had used three false witnesses against him: Bobby Whittaker, John Neuman, and Mary West. Conahan said that in his initial statement to police, Whittaker said that Conahan had come by the trailer looking for Montgomery, found him there, and spent forty-five minutes talking with him, and that Conahan had come back on at least two other occasions. When he was officially deposed, Conahan said, Whittaker changed his story to say that Conahan had only come to the trailer one time, not finding Montgomery there—the same story he told on the witness stand.

He was angry at his attorneys for not following up on this point. "I was led to believe that during the defense portion of the trial, that they would call Mr. Whittaker back and expose these things—which they did not do."

As for Mary West, Richard Montgomery's mother: "She did lie under oath, and I can understand why she did. It's her son, and she felt that she needed to get some type of revenge or whatever it is."

John Neuman, Conahan's Lee County Jail cell mate, had traded his false testimony for lowering a first-degree murder charge to manslaughter, halving his prison sentence, Conahan charged.

The interviewer said, "What was going through your mind when you were getting the final sentencing? Emotionally, did you go through anything there?"

"Well, it wasn't surprising—it's what I expected, so it was not a surprise," Conahan said. "My emotions I've dealt with pretty much in the privacy of the jail, in my own cell."

Conahan spoke of being arrested for Stanley Burden's sexual assault and attempted murder. "I was shocked, because I knew I was innocent. And I felt that: how could they arrest me for something like that?"

"You admitted to the police about having a bondage fantasy. . . . What did you admit to them?"

"Well, it came up toward the end of the [5/31/96] interview at the Holiday Inn, and I admitted that, yeah, you know, I've fantasized about bondage before. But I have never acted out on that fantasy. And I certainly did not act out with Mr. Montgomery, to the point of murder, or anyone else. So that's basically what I told 'em."

"But do you think that was the m/o of the killer in this case, whoever it was? That they were acting out a bondage fantasy?"

"I couldn't say."

"What about Stanley Burden? Tell us about him."

"Well, it's quite obvious something happened to Stanley Burden," Conahan said. "I certainly did not hurt Stanley Burden, or have anything to do with that incident Stanley Burden was in. I had, as I said at the trial, met Mr. Burden, and he was hustling for money. And we did have a quick sexual episode. And then I returned him to where I met him and picked him up.

"Stanley Burden is a habitual, admitted habitual liar."

Had Conahan asked Burden about doing a nude bondage scene for money?

"I don't remember, actually, if I did or not. I may have. I may have said, Well you know, maybe you would be interested, or— I really don't remember if I had said anything like that to him at all," Conahan said.

"Did you ever choke him?"

"Not at all. We engaged in oral sex, and then I dropped him back off at Lyons Park."

The interviewer said, "In the Montgomery case, your own lawyers alluded to autoerotic asphyxia as a possibility for Montgomery's death. Is that possible? That you got carried away with a bondage fantasy and killed him accidentally, and you didn't want to admit it?"

Conahan said, "I've never engaged in bondage with anyone, and most certainly did not engage in any type of bondage beyond fantasy with Mr. Burden or anyone else. A fantasy's a fantasy—you know, I didn't act it out. It's not an uncommon thing."

Conahan noted the toll taken since his initial arrest. Both his parents died during his first year in jail, at about the time he was charged with murder. His sister had broken off contact with him. "There's not a lot of my family left. That leaves my aunt and then the Lindes, which are also my family."

He recalled his early years with fondness. "I was always a, believe it or not, a sensitive person, and very aware of other people's feelings. And my mom was, also. We had a good family life. We'd go on vacations, camping trips, boating. A lot of outdoor type of activities."

Asked for his reaction to the revelation that he'd been under intense police surveillance for fifty-three days, Conahan said, "Well, I didn't have anything to hide by being followed. I was surprised, and probably a little shocked. . . ."

During that surveillance, he was caught on tape soliciting two undercover police officers for nude bondage scenes. The interviewer noted the contradiction with Conahan's statement earlier in the interview, when he'd denied that he ever tried to "act out" a bondage fantasy.

Conahan said, "There was a police officer that was panhandling for money, for work, that I did have contact with. . . . I did talk to him about having sex, sexual favors. I did mention bondage."

"If you were looking for the killer of Richard Montgomery, what would you be looking for?"

Conahan named a male relative of Bobby Whittaker's, whom he alleged had been involved in a mutilation murder. He spoke about his innocence, saying that the exhaustive, expensive police investigation had failed to turn up any hard evidence against him. "They didn't find anything. They didn't find the murder weapon; they didn't find any DNA; they didn't find any hair; they didn't find any instruments that they were believed were used in the murder. They did find a camera, some film, some clothesline that was in my car, camera film in my bedroom. I did have my kitchen stuff, where there was some steak knives that I had purchased. . . .

"Basically what the case boils down to—the fibers; a paint chip; the perjured testimony of Whittaker; the mother's perjured statement; John Neuman's statement—perjured statement. And Mr. Burden's statements—who's a habitual liar."

"So what happened here—what do we have here? What is this a case of?"

"This is a case of someone being arrested for a murder they did not commit. I could understand how, in general, they may have thought that I was a murderer, or involved in these crimes."

Conahan wasn't too happy about his lawyers, either. "Personally, they did not do their job at all. Mark Ahlbrand, I had problems with him throughout. And Paul Sullivan, but specifically Mark Ahlbrand."

"Do you think they believe you're innocent?"

"Well, they say they do."

"Who else believes that?"

"I think anybody who takes the time to really look into this case," Conahan said.

Again, as in his courtroom testimony, nothing was revealed.

Police never gave up trying to identify John Doe Number Three, found on March 7, 1996. They had his fingerprints, which they kept checking against entries in computerized data bases. Three years and millions of entries later, they hit a match. Ironically, it came more or less from next door, from the Charlotte County Sheriff's Office, who had the dead man's prints on file for an arrest for shoplifting. He was William John Malaragno, Jr., from Cleveland, Ohio, a free-spirited type drifting from job to job, who'd somehow managed to land in Florida, into the clutches of the Hog Trail Killer.

That brought to three the number of victims with some sort of connection to Ohio. Stanley Burden, Richard Montgomery, and now Malaragno were all originally from Ohio. Was it coincidence, or some sort of triggering cue in the killer's psyche?

Another question: what happened to the body

parts taken from the scenes? Investigators theorized that they were not kept as trophies, but were disposed of by the killer, possibly in Dumpsters. One variation is that he got rid of them by putting them in biohazard bags, disposing of them with other medical waste at Charlotte Regional Medical Center.

Then there were the Polaroids. What happened to the film he shot at the various crime scenes? Did he photograph the victims after death, collecting "snuff" photos? If Conahan indeed kept a secret stash of such photos, police never found it, and they looked hard for it.

Police are also looking into other murders that Conahan might have committed prior to moving to Florida.

Florida v. *Brancaccio:*

"Prescription for Murder"

The Crime

On Friday, June 11, 1993, at seven o'clock, Mollie Mae Frazier, eighty-one, set out on one of her usual evening walks. A white-haired widow who lived alone, Frazier was a quiet, friendly person and regular churchgoer. She liked to walk through the neighborhood at sundown. Friends had expressed some concern about her walking alone by herself just before dark, but she'd laughed and said, "Oh, I live in a wonderful neighborhood. I'm perfectly safe."

Frazier resided in a house on Southwest Cedar Cove in St. Lucie West, an attractive, upscale suburb of south Florida's Port St. Lucie, site of the spring training camp of the New York Mets baseball team. The Heatherwood Estates area where she lived housed some retirees like herself, but was predominantly a place for well-to-do families.

One such were the Brancaccios, living a few
streets away from Frazier in a palatial house on
nearby Moonlite Cove.

Eugene "Gene" Brancaccio, and his wife, Adelina "Lina," both in their early forties, were an
American success story. Originally from Naples,
Italy, they'd come to south Florida and worked
hard building up a business, the Roma West com-
bination bakery and pizza place that was one of
the most popular in town. Their column-fronted
Heatherwood house had cost $237,000. They had
three sons, Albert, Salvatore, and the youngest,
Victor. More than once, police had been called
to the house to cool off a domestic dispute. But
the family was respected as successful business
people and hard workers.

On June 11, young Victor Brancaccio had had a
bad day at the landscaping company where he
worked. Brancaccio, sixteen, 5'3," 140 pounds, had
a poor academic record, but did well in music and
boxing. He'd dropped out of high school to work
for the landscaper. Coming home, he'd gotten into
a shouting match with his mother. The ostensible
reason for the fight, while seemingly small and ri-
diculous, spoke volumes. Brancaccio wanted to
send out for pizza for dinner, but not Roma West
pizza, the pizza made by his family. He wanted pizza
from another pizzeria, one of the competition. This
quite naturally enraged his mother.

Things got hot. Brancaccio later said that he'd
gone out because he was afraid that if he stayed
in, he would have hit his mother. He stormed out

of the house, but not without his Walkman personal stereo player, from which he was inseparable. He also paused to pick up a Lazer Tag toy gun. This was not an ordinary toy gun, but an electronic replica gun, a plastic model of a 9mm Beretta semiautomatic pistol, a simulation whose likeness to the real thing could fool cops and civilians alike, with potentially lethal results.

Toy gun in his pocket, Brancaccio left the house at about seven o'clock. Pumping through the earphones of his Walkman was a tape of gangster rap music—the kind of music he liked to listen to when he was angry.

A little while later, neighbor Jan Simcsuk drove along Heatherwood's main street, taking her teenage son Jesse somewhere. On one side of the street, set back from and running parallel to it, was a berm, a low grassy ridge built into the landscape to serve as a noise barrier. Planted on top of it was a row of hedges. On the far side of the berm lay a vast cleared tract, a development subdivision waiting for construction to begin. The berm hid it from view of the road.

Driving by, Simcsuk witnessed a curious tableau. Walking along the road was Mollie Frazier, a white-haired woman in a blouse, blue shorts, and sneakers. Close behind her was a teenage male wearing a Walkman and headphones, waving his arms in the air. He wore overalls and was bare-chested, his shirt stuffed in his back pocket. On his feet were white hightop sneakers.

A woman and her grandson out for a walk together, was Simcsuk's first thought. How nice. Her son said, "That kid's a jerk. That's Victor Brancaccio. I'd like to beat him up."

"Don't be silly," Simcsuk said, driving on. Glancing back in her rearview mirror, she saw Brancaccio closing on Mollie Frazier, waving his hands in the air. She thought he was making hand gestures to the music.

Later, she would wonder about what exactly she'd seen, and if she'd properly interpreted it. Brancaccio had been quite close behind Frazier, almost at her heels, but she'd looked straight ahead, unaware of, or ignoring him.

On Sunday, June 13, concerned about Mollie Frazier's failure to attend that day's church service and Sunday school class as she routinely did, friend Shirley Hoy made several calls that afternoon to Frazier's home. The phone rang and rang, but there was no answer. Hoy was getting worried.

Sunday night, at 11 P.M., at the Port St. Lucie police station, Sergeant Donald Kryak, road patrol supervisor on the four-to-midnight shift, was looking forward to going off duty in an hour, when the receptionist told him that there was a gentleman who wanted to report finding a body.

Kryak and another officer went to the front lobby, where they found twentyish Larry Winchester, his sister Lynette, seventeen, his girlfriend, and her baby, all visibly upset. Larry Winchester did most of the talking. Kryak asked him to accompany him to where the body was, requesting that Winchester's sister and girlfriend remain at the station.

Kryak and Winchester got in Kryak's police car and drove away, followed by the other duty sergeant in another car. Along the way, Kryak radioed for a K-9 team to meet him at the scene, in case they needed help in finding the body. As it turned out, that would not be necessary.

The police cars rolled through the moonlit streets of different subdivisions. It was a place of expensive homes, lawns and gardens, and minimal crime, a near-zero-crime oasis. That was important, because in June 1993, the state was experiencing a violent crime wave that included carjackings, riots, drug gang shootouts, and homicides. Such sordid aspects of the modern world seemed far away here in the serene nightscape of St. Lucie West, where the police blotter mainly featured burglaries and petty crimes.

The cars entered the Heatherwood area. Kryak left the main road behind, entering a subdivision in the process of development. The street grid was laid out, lots had been cleared, but building had yet to begin.

Winchester directed the cops to a paved road ending in the cul-de-sac of Crabapple Cove. The police cars parked where they could best deploy their headlights to light up the area. Beyond the cul-de-sac was a low rise which blocked the lights, screening what lay behind it. If a body was there, they couldn't see it.

The lawmen and Winchester got out of the cars.

It was a lonely scene—no houses nearby, dark, the sky filled with bright moonlight. Winchester and Kryak started toward the rise, the second officer following. The police officers had their flashlights out, beams lancing and sweeping across the landscape. The trio walked about seventy-five yards, mounting the top of the rise.

On the other side, the ground fell away, dipping into a hollow, a gully that lay below the level of the surrounding ground. In the middle of an open field cleared of trees and brush lay the body of an elderly female.

The corpse had been painted bright red.

A veteran with thirteen years of law enforcement experience, ten as a uniformed cop and three as a detective, Sergeant Kryak had seen many dead bodies before—those who'd died of natural causes and others who'd died violently. He was expecting to find a body in the gully. But a red-painted, elderly female corpse—that was shocking, bizarre.

The body lay sprawled on the ground. Only the exposed skin areas had been painted, not the clothes. This was no light overspray: her body was literally coated and covered with red paint. Bright red. Face, arms, hands, legs, were all painted.

It was a macabre, unforgettable image, one of the damnedest things Kryak had ever seen.

There was more. What also leaped out, after the shock of the red paint, was that someone had tried to burn the corpse. The lower part of her body was splayed, vividly displaying the effects of fire.

There were no small burns, like those from a

cigarette. These were major scorch marks. Her lap, groin, and the top of her legs were noticeably burned and her clothing was charred. She'd been lit on fire. No doubt that this fire had been intentionally set.

This was not a fresh corpse, there were clear signs of decomposition and insect infestation and the south Florida wet heat had taken its toll. Even through the red paint, there were indications of significant trauma. She'd been beaten. To what extent it was difficult to tell, but there was clearly trauma to the head. The face was lacerated, the nose broken, and the head was bruised. The chest had sustained a massive crushing injury that had virtually collapsed the entire right side.

Kryak told *Court TV* of his feelings at finding the body. "First thing you ask is, why? You get a sick feeling in your stomach. You just can't believe that one human can do this to somebody else. It wasn't one those, 'This is so gruesome I'm going to throw up.' It was just the senselessness of it. It just turns your stomach.

"It was strange . . . unique. Strange. It was an elderly female with paint and burn marks. That's the image that sticks with me, as graphic as the paint, bright red paint on these exposed areas. And then the burns and the burned clothing. That's an image that's going to stick with me forever."

Kryak and the other officer had seen enough. Being first on the scene, they sealed off the immediate area with yellow evidence tape and called detectives.

Later that night, at about 12:30 A.M., as detectives and evidence collectors swarmed the site, Kryak and his supervisor eyed a vehicle which they'd noticed hovering around the scene, a place that was generally not well traveled at night. The car drove back and forth. Something wasn't right. Kryak and the other officer got in a car, following the other car and pulling it over.

In the car were two Port St. Lucie men, Giacomo "Jack" Zaccheo, seventeen, and Angel Pellot, eighteen. As it turned out, they had some valuable information. They weren't eager to share it with police, but they did. They knew the body was out there. A name came up as they talked: Victor Brancaccio.

Kryak noted, "As a member of the department, you get reports and on occasion you'll see repeat calls, a particular name. . . . We were familiar with Victor and the fact that he had been involved with the police before."

At around eleven-thirty Sunday night, Port St. Lucie Police Department Detective Sergeant Scott Beck was notified at home of the finding of the body of an elderly woman. He went to the scene, where he spoke to Larry Winchester. Before the night was over, Beck had interviewed four of the principals: Larry Winchester, Lynette Winchester, Jack Zaccheo, and Angel Pellot, all of whom were acquaintances or friends of Victor Brancaccio.

Brancaccio was not entirely unknown to police.

In October 1992, he'd gotten into a fight with another high school student, breaking his nose. More recently, on April 16, 1993, while attending a party, Brancaccio, unable to buy beer from a convenience store, stole a six-pack and got caught. He told the arresting officer that he wanted to kill himself and his parents. Instead of going to jail, he went into the New Horizons crisis center for two days. After that, his parents had put him in Savannas Hospital for a thirty-day stay, with a release date of May 11.

Beck learned that on Friday, June 11, Brancaccio had had some sort of altercation with an elderly woman, that he'd struck and killed her, that he'd bragged about it to a number of friends, ultimately taking two of them on Saturday afternoon to view the body. None of his friends had believed him, except for the two who'd seen the body. Later, Brancaccio tried to burn the body and failed, then spray painted it to cover up the evidence.

A neighborhood canvassing soon led to the identification of the elderly woman. Mollie Frazier was no longer among the missing.

On Monday, June 14, at about 9 A.M., clad in a blue sweatshirt and jeans, Victor Brancaccio left the house and got into a vehicle owned by the landscaper for whom he worked. Police swooped down, arresting him. When he asked why he was being arrested, the arresting officers said they didn't know. He was handcuffed, put into the back of a police car and taken away.

A search warrant had been obtained from a Port St. Lucie County judge, allowing investigators to search the Brancaccio house, which they began doing.

Arriving at the station at nine-thirty, Brancaccio asked if his parents had been notified. He was told it was being taken care of. At ten o'clock his Miranda rights were read to him and his interview with Detective Scott Beck began. Beck thought Brancaccio's demeanor was "calm," as initially he denied knowing what it was all about, lying during the first few minutes of the interview. Beck told some untruths of his own, saying that there were witnesses who'd seen Brancaccio going toward the crime scene with a can of spray paint, and that the spray painting had had the opposite effect to what Brancaccio had intended. Instead of covering up the fingerprint evidence, the paint had brought it out, enhancing it, Beck lied. The trick worked. Brancaccio said, "Listen, I've got to tell you the truth."

He said that after the argument with his mother, he'd been walking through the neighborhood, trying to cool down. His music was blasting through his earphones, hard gangster rap. On came Dr. Dre's "Stranded on Death Row," and Brancaccio couldn't keep still, he had to react. He was stalking along, shouting out the profanity-laced lyrics.

Then he crossed paths with an old woman. Although Frazier and Brancaccio lived within a few streets of each other, there is no evidence that they knew each other. As Brancaccio told it, the old lady had started upbraiding him for his conduct, for shouting obscenities. In his version, she bad-mouthed him, calling him "white trash" and "low class" and saying that he didn't belong in this high-class neighborhood. He'd had enough. He punched her in the face, bruising and cutting her over the right eye. She said, "I didn't know you were this kind of person." She took out a handkerchief or tissue, mopping her blood, then offering it to him so he could wipe her blood off his hand.

He said, "Bitch, do you have AIDS?"

He was in trouble now. He decided to beat her until she couldn't tell on him, until she forgot what had happened. He led her up over the berm and down the other side, into a hollow, a cleared, sandy flat. The locale was about 200 yards away from the Brancaccio house.

Now he could do what he had to without anybody coming along and seeing. Brancaccio said he hit Frazier with the gun, startling Beck, who hadn't known that a firearm was involved. Brancaccio explained that it was a replica plastic toy gun. He'd struck Frazier with it in the head so hard that the gun flew into pieces. He then beat her head with his Walkman. She dropped to the ground and he kicked her in the head, stomach, and chest.

He followed her down, beating her, hammering her with his fists, feet, knees. He beat her and crushed her and left her there twitching. According to the medical examiner, Frazier could not have lived more than a few minutes with the kind of damage she'd sustained.

Hearing what he thought was a car, Brancaccio ran home, leaving his Walkman at the scene. He went about his normal routine, calling a friend, arranging for her to pick him up later, which she did, arriving at 9 P.M. They went to another friend's house, where they engaged in typical teenage activities, wrestling around, watching TV, and eating pizza. Brancaccio told them he'd beaten up an old lady, but they didn't believe him. They thought he was just making it up, trying to be the center of attention. He said they were right, he was just kidding, making it all up.

The next day, Saturday, about 9 A.M., Brancaccio went back down into the field. The body was below ground-level sightlines and had remained undiscovered since the night before. Mollie Frazier was still there. Brancaccio told Beck that for some reason, he'd thought that Frazier was still alive. He said something like, "Lady, it's me, the same guy; do you need help?" She didn't answer so he said, "Well, fuck you, bitch."

He retrieved his Walkman, the main reason he'd gone there. He picked up some of the biggest pieces of the shattered plastic gun, disposing of them by throwing them into a nearby lake.

Seeing an oncoming car that he recognized, he flagged it down. Angel Pellot, the driver, worked for the Brancaccios. They went to the piz-

zeria, where Brancaccio hooked up with another
family employee, Jack Zaccheo, and his girlfriend,
Lynette Winchester. After work, they went shopping for car parts. On the way back, Brancaccio
said he would show them the body. He directed
Zaccheo to pull into the Crabapple Cove cul-de-
sac. They got out, went over the rise, and down
into the bowl, where Mollie Frazier's body lay.
They got back in the car and Zaccheo drove Brancaccio home, dropping him off.

Brancaccio decided to get rid of the evidence
by burning it. He returned to the lot, carrying
some newspapers. They'd do for kindling. He put
the crumpled newspapers at the dead woman's
crotch and set it afire with matches, inflicting the
scorching which had been so apparent to Kryak.

The area of the body which was set ablaze
caused some investigators to speculate that Brancaccio might have lit the fire to destroy evidence
of some sexual assault. The speculation was
heightened by a comment made by Brancaccio
to Zaccheo, saying of Frazier, "She was so
knocked out, I could have fucked her." But there
was no hard evidence to back up the charge of
sexual assault and no charges were ever filed
against Brancaccio for this.

The damage the fire had done was minimal
compared to what Brancaccio had hoped it would
do. Clearly he needed something else. Fingerprints worried him. He had to protect himself.
He went home, returning with a can of red spray
paint. Thinking it would destroy the evidence, he

spray painted Frazier's body red. That was the last contact he'd had with the body, he told Beck. After that, he went home.

Beck knew the rest: Jack Zaccheo and Lynette Winchester were unnerved. Knowing Victor Brancaccio had committed murder could be a scary proposition. Knowing that he knew they knew he had was even worse. After all, he'd already killed once. Who knew what other ideas he might get in his head? At nine-thirty on Sunday night, Lynette Winchester took her brother, Larry, to see the body. He went to police, taking his sister and girlfriend with him.

Beck found Brancaccio a cold one. "It was a very cold, very calculated, very mean-spirited type of thing. I deal with crime all the time. I deal with violent people all the time. Victor isn't only violent, he's evil.

"It appeared to me that he was a star in a play. He actually enjoyed the attention, that this was something that he was actually enjoying and thriving on the events that were occurring. I think in his mind he kind of felt like he was the big man now, that he was the center of attention, that he he had actually done something noteworthy."

With the Mollie Frazier slaying in the news, along with Victor Brancaccio's picture, witness Jan Simcsuk contacted police, telling them that she and her son had seen the two walking together along the roadway on Friday night. In hindsight, what had seemed like a woman taking a walk with her grandson was repainted in sinister touches as a prelude to a fatal encounter, taking place just minutes, before the murder.

She'd looked back in her rearview mirror and seen Brancaccio closing on Mollie Frazier, hands flailing in the air. Perhaps instead of keeping time to the music, he'd been making threatening gestures toward her as he closed in.

Witnesses Jack Zaccheo and Lynette Winchester expressed fear of the Brancaccio family to police. Beck told *Court TV*, "They were afraid of the family, afraid of the family contacts, and afraid of what Victor might do to them."

Rumors were floating around that the family was linked to organized crime, although investigators and reporters alike were never able to confirm such links. Perhaps it was a case of vicious ethnic stereotyping. Still despite official denials, there was a general feeling abroad that the Brancaccios were bad people to cross.

THE TRIAL

The Brancaccio family hired attorney Juan Torres to defend Victor. Torres first floated a novel defense, that Gene and Lina Brancaccio were first cousins and that son Victor might have suffered from genetically borne mental defects. Word soon came from the defense camp of a new strategy. The defense was going to claim that Brancaccio was not guilty by reason of temporary insanity. He'd committed the crime in a state of involuntary intoxication, caused by Zoloft, the prescription antidepressant drug that he'd been taking at the time of the murder.

While at Savannas Hospital in April 1993, Victor Brancaccio had been given Zoloft to treat his depression, and he'd been regularly taking it since. Zoloft was one of the leading antidepressant medicines, and there was no record of violence associated with it. Still, there was an exploitable legal angle there somewhere. In the early 1990s, a study reported finding suicidal feelings among a certain small percentage of Prozac users and the floodgates were opened for a wave of lawsuits claiming damages against Prozac for its responsibility for suicides and murders. None of those suits had ever succeeded, but that didn't deter fresh ones from being filed.

Now Zoloft had been brought onstage in the Mollie Frazier murder. Did the drug cause violence in a certain number of patients? The state was going to put Victor Brancaccio on trial. The defense was going to put Zoloft on trial. Torres started lining up medical experts to investigate the effects of Zoloft on violent behavior.

It was a bold defense move and an expensive one. Expert witnesses are costly and the defense couldn't get enough of them. The legal bills were crippling. The Brancaccios began experiencing serious cash flow problems. They missed some payments on the mortgage and lost the Moonlite Cove house, moving into a smaller one. In the year and a half following Victor's arrest, the family lost its house and business, and failed making payments on a department store charge card and two bank credit cards.

The money crisis reached a head in early 1995, about a year after the crime. As the case was about to go to trial, defense attorney Torres asked for a continuance, saying that he lacked the money to hire all his psychiatric experts to testify about Brancaccio's mental state. The judge agreed to postpone the trial. The family needed to immediately raise $75,000 it didn't have, with no prospects of raising even a small part of the money.

The Brancaccios filed a civil suit for damages against Savannas Hospital, saying they had released Victor Brancaccio prematurely and that the Zoloft prescribed for him by a staff doctor had combined with his physical and emotional state, triggering Mollie Frazier's brutal murder. The family was pretty much out of cash at this point, and the suit was seen by some as a last-ditch attempt to recoup some of their losses. The civil suit was delayed pending the outcome of the criminal trial.

A week later, on February 2, 1995, Gene and Lina Brancaccio were watching a Sunday mass service on television, when Lina Brancaccio decided to check the five-dollar Quick Pick ticket her husband had bought on Friday, against the winning LOTTO numbers she'd jotted down the night before. Gene Brancaccio was a faithful LOTTO player who'd been playing the game since its start. The Quick Pick ticket numbers were randomly drawn by computer.

All six numbers matched. A win!

The Brancaccio's share of the jackpot totaled $2.8 million. They held a press conference, Lina Brancaccio telling reporters, "It's a miracle." Gene Brancaccio said that they'd use the money to pay for their son Victor's defense.

It was a crazy coincidence, as fantastic as anything out of the *Arabian Nights,* the kind of thing that'd be scornfully dismissed as too corny even for Hollywood, but being true, had no need to conform to the laws of logic. The Brancaccios had experienced crushing lows and vaunting highs. The bad news was that their son was on trial for murder; the good news was that they now had a couple of million dollars to spend on his defense.

That was unwelcome news to many in Port St. Lucie who now had reason to fear that Victor Brancaccio would someday walk the streets again as a free man. The result was a sea change in the emotional atmosphere surrounding the case. Before, there had been a kind of tight silence from the community. During Brancaccio's bail hearing, the prosecution had said that there would have been more witnesses from the area to testify that Brancaccio was a threat to the community, except that they were afraid of the family.

Now, fury started to rise. The Brancaccios received death threats, callers phoning to warn that if Victor Brancaccio was somehow set free, they'd "burn him on the cross." Unrelated people named Brancaccio started getting unlisted phone numbers.

Such fury could only mount at the announcement that, to defend Victor, the family was retaining one of America's best-known trial lawyers, Miami attorney Roy Black. Black, fifty, had first come to national prominence as a television commentator during the trial of O. J. Simpson. He'd scored notable victories on behalf of such clients as William Kennedy Smith, charged with rape; actor Kelsey Grammer, television's *Frasier,* accused of having sex with a fifteen-year-old girl; sportscaster Marv Albert, charged with sexual misconduct; and a Miami police officer charged with the killing of a black youth, whose acquittal sparked bloody riots. Black, a Coral Gables resident, had recently married a woman who had been a juror on the Kennedy Smith case. They'd met after the trial was over.

Black described himself as being committed to the defense of "the unpopular, the politically incorrect, and even the publicly despised." Miami prosecutor Michael Band, defeated by Black in the Kennedy Smith rape case, said of his high-priced legal adversary, "Roy represents people who can afford him. You're basically innocent until proven broke."

* * *

Victor Brancaccio was charged with the first-degree murder and kidnapping of Mollie Frazier. Murder One, because it was premeditated—Brancaccio had made a conscious decision to kill her. Kidnapping, because he'd taken Frazier behind the berm, into the lot, against her will. That trip behind the berm was the linchpin of the prosecution's strategy. The prosecutors were Lynn Park, assistant state attorney for the 19th Judicial Circuit and attorney in charge of the Indian River County State Attorney's Office; and Assistant State Attorney Lawrence Mirman. For the defense, Roy Black was joined by co-counsel Tim Schulz.

Because of adverse publicity, the trial was moved from Port St. Lucie to Vero Beach's Indian River County Courthouse thirty miles away. The proceedings began on Friday, January 8, 1999. Victor Brancaccio, who'd been sixteen at the time of the crime, was now twenty-one. He'd spent the intervening years in jail, waiting to go to trial.

Prosecutor Lawrence Mirman's opening hit the facts of the crime hard. Brancaccio had an argument with his mother. He decided to go outside and take a walk. Before leaving, he selected two items to take with him: his Walkman personal stereo, loaded with a cassette tape, and a toy gun, a replica of a .9mm semiautomatic handgun. He went outside, bopping down the street, through the neighborhood, getting into the gangster rap, waving his hands and shouting along with the lyrics.

Then he made contact with Mollie Frazier.

That was how the prosecution put it, "made contact." There was a lot of doubt about Brancaccio's version of how he'd crossed paths with Mollie Frazier. Frazier's friends and pastor recalled her as shy and reserved, disbelieving that she would ever have confronted Brancaccio, no less upbraided him as "low class" and "white trash." It simply wasn't in character.

Reverend Jim Wingate, pastor of Frazier's church, said sadly, "Mollie was a quiet person. She was thoughtful and very shy. A little hard to get to know, but once you did, she was very congenial, friendly. Once you made a friend of her, she was your friend for life."

He added, "I understand that she was brutally beaten. You think about the fear that was going through her heart and through her mind, trying to get away from a young man, hoping against hope somehow that maybe she could get away from him. Those moments are horrible moments to think about."

Wingate also knew of the Brancaccios, and said "Often we went there to get their subs. Served one of the best subs in Port St. Lucie. They seemed to be good people. Good business people, an asset to the community."

Prosecutors and investigators thought it more likely that Brancaccio had gone out looking for trouble. That was why he'd paused to take the replica gun with him, a toy that could easily pass for the real thing. By that argument, Frazier just happened to be unlucky enough to cross his

path, but it could have been someone else, anyone else. That she'd scolded and bad-mouthed
him was just another of the defendant's self-serv-
ing stories, designed to, if not make him look
good, at least paint him a little less blackly, suggesting that there was at least some kind of in-
citement that triggered him off.

Mirman said, "Mrs. Frazier was walking in front
of him. In response to having contact with her,
he chose to punch her in the face, slug an eighty-
one-year-old woman in the face. The defendant
made a choice, that was that he was afraid to get
in trouble. So he made a decision to take Mrs.
Frazier into a field where no one could see them,
for the purpose of beating her to a point where
she could not remember what had happened."

He attacked, hitting her so hard with the replica gun that it broke into pieces, so hard that
one of the pieces had one of her hairs stuck to
it. He beat her with his fist, hitting so hard that
there were four separate areas of trauma, each of
which would have caused death. He stomped her,
crushed her ribs and chest.

He went home and immediately started covering up his crime, the prosecution charged. The
cover-up began when his mother asked him
where he'd been and he told her he'd gone to
McDonald's. "As he was lying to his mother, Mollie Frazier was dying in a field. She lived anywhere
from a half hour to an hour after the beating."

Victor Brancaccio went on with his life, making
plans for Friday night fun. He hung out with

some girls, watched TV, ordered pizza, while he joked about killing an "old lady." The next day, he tried to burn the body, then spray painted it.

"He had contact with his friends. He bragged about what he did. He said, 'She was giving me shit, so I beat her to death.' His words," Mirman said. "Let the jury hear more of the defendant's words, when he showed his friends the body: 'What, you're not going to hang out with me?'; 'Feel bad? A little, but I'm cold-hearted.'; 'Maybe I should get a lawn mower and cut her up.' "

Mirman continued, "He motions to this girl [Lynette Winchester], 'She's all red now.' Finally, in describing his beating of eighty-one-year-old Mollie Frazier, he said, 'She was strong for an old bitch. She was so knocked out, I could have fucked her.'

"He admitted he punched her, took her into the field, knew what he was doing and that it was wrong. . . . He beat her over the head, beating and terrorizing her, committing kidnapping, and when she was killed that became first-degree murder."

Roy Black was solemn, more sorrowful than angry. He began by saying he didn't dispute the horrific nature of the crime. "There is no question that what happened here is a horrible act," he told the jury. "You'll be horrified."

What happened to Mollie Frazier was wrong; there was no way to condone it. No one condoned it. It was a tragedy. But that was the point. What made it horrible was what made Victor Brancaccio not guilty by reason of insanity. "People say, 'How could somebody in their right mind do something like this?' The answer is, he was not in his right mind."

Black said that Victor Brancaccio's actions were "the antithesis of cover-up." Instead, he'd gone around telling his friends what he'd done. He had a compulsion to confess. He goes home and calls a friend and says, "I can't believe it, I think I hurt an old lady." He hitches a ride from another, and before getting in the car, says, "I think I hurt an old lady." Then he shows the blood on his sneaker.

Brancaccio is suggestible. Others, particularly Jack Zaccheo, influenced him to try to get rid of the evidence by burning the body. Brancaccio tells stories. Maybe he even thinks they're true. He told different versions of his story to police and friends. In one version, in the middle of the beating, Mollie Frazier offers him a handkerchief to wipe her blood off his hand.

Black said, "You cannot rely on what he says."

And you can't rely on police to play fair, not when they're trying to get Brancaccio to incriminate himself. Right from the start they dealt in bad faith, taking unfair advantage. Instead of arresting Brancaccio at home when his parents were there, they waited until he was outside, in his boss's car, before arresting him.

Florida law says the parents must be notified,

but police "make no effort, deliberately decide not to do so. They don't want the parents to be alerted prior to the search of the house." The police report records this exchange between Victor Brancaccio and police: "Have my parents been notified?" "We are taking care of it."

Black said, "We know that because it is in the report. I think they wanted to get him alone to interrogate him. You will hear it when you listen to the tape. It's obvious from the beginning Sergeant Beck knows this man has just been released from the hospital." Black accused the police of leading Brancaccio on, "not that he didn't do these things, but they are going to try to show that he was in his right mind."

What was that mind like?

The killing of Mollie Frazier "was a frenzied attack without any reason between two people who do not know each other, the most senseless kind of a killing. How did it happen? Why? Is there some cause, something that's happened to him that would explain it?

"I believe that there is," Black said, launching a quick rundown of Brancaccio's background, laying the groundwork for the defense's medical/psychiatric argument. Born in 1977, Brancaccio was premature, underweight. At age two, he fell face down into a pond and stopped breathing for about four minutes. He'd been rushed to the hospital to be treated for a dangerous buildup of gases in his blood.

Black said, "People treating him believe that

these events caused him organic brain damage. He had to repeat the first grade, second grade." His I.Q. tested borderline retarded. More recently, he'd been diagnosed as severely depressed. On April 16, 1993, while drunk, he had stolen a six-pack of beer from a store. After two days in a crisis center, his parents put him in Savannas Hospital in Port St. Lucie for twenty-three days.

When first admitted, he was diagnosed for depression. His affect (facial expression) was flat, expressionless, withdrawn. He was cooperative, sad, wanted to go home. Then on April 30, twelve days into his stay, he began taking prescribed doses of Zoloft, an antidepressant medicine. As the drug took effect, his behavior changed, going from flat to hyperactive. He was labeled a "class clown, with a potential for violence . . . angry and fearful of going home."

Black said, "There is an incredible change in his personality when he starts taking medication. He's bouncing off the walls. For days he is begging them not to let him out of the hospital.

"We are not saying Zoloft should not be used. However, there are people who cannot take this kind of medication. It is a small percentage." Brancaccio was not a normal person, he suffered from organic brain damage. Somewhere in the mysteries of brain chemistry, where neurons fire synapses and neurotransmitters spark brain activity, there was a deadly short circuit in Brancaccio's brain when he was taking Zoloft.

"We don't know what is going to happen with

people like that. . . . When he was released, this
young man was a time bomb. There is no premeditation here, he didn't know this woman. . . .
You will see that this is a severely brain-damaged
man, who ought to be found not guilty by reason
of insanity," Black said, ending his opening remarks.

After recess, the state began presenting its case,
first calling Larry Winchester, who'd led police
to the body. On Lynn Park's direct examination,
Winchester said that on Sunday, June 13, at about
nine-thirty, his younger sister Lynette, with whom
he had a good relationship, told him that she'd
seen a dead body in the field off Crabapple Cove.
He believed what she'd told him, but he had to
see for himself. He, his girlfriend, her infant son,
and Lynette went for a drive in St. Lucie West,
going to the scene.

He parked the car, got out. It was dark. He
climbed to the top of the berm and looked for
a body, but couldn't see one. He got back in the
car and drove around to the far side of the field
to a cul-de-sac. There were paved streets, but no
houses. He drove across the field, headlights on.
The beams picked out a body, and its arms and
legs. Winchester went to the police station and
told Sergeant Kryak what he'd seen, leading him
to the body.

Officer Don Kryak, since promoted to lieutenant, took up the narrative from there, telling of

the finding of the red-painted corpse. Park said, "Did you and another officer stop a car that came around? Why did you stop it?"

"It had been driving in an unusual and suspicious manner so we stopped it," Kryak said. In the vehicle were Jack Zaccheo and Angel Pellot, who were detained for questioning.

Tim Schulz, on cross-examination, said, "Based upon discussions with Larry Winchester, you had a suspect in mind?"

Kryak said, "A suspect had been suggested."

"That was Brancaccio?"

"Yes."

"You'd heard that name before?"

"Yes."

An eight-and-a-half-year veteran of the Port St. Lucie Police Department, Crime Scene Investigator Robert Fitch collected evidence at the field: tissue paper with blood on it, peppermint candy, pieces of a black-plastic toy handgun, burnt newspaper and, of course, the body itself. The bloody tissue paper was found nine feet away from the body. Pieces of the gun were also found in a nearby lake.

Defense Counsel Tim Schulz was interested in the circumstances of Brancaccio's arrest. Fitch said that when officers took the defendant out of the truck, "He said over and over, you got the wrong man."

Fitch had also measured the distance between the body and Brancaccio's house, about 200 yards. Following standard procedure, a sex-crime-kit test was made on the body, with negative results.

Port St. Lucie Police Department Detective James Howie, on Lawrence Mirman's direct, told of searching the Brancaccio house, beginning at about 10:45 A.M. In a closet, he'd found a pair of Fila high-top sneakers belonging to the defendant, and two red spray-paint cans. A third red spray-paint can was found on a shelf in the garage. Two cans were Dutchboy–brand paint, the third Wal-Mart.

Mirman said, "Did you see anything unusual on the sneakers?"

Howie said he noticed a reddish stain, possibly blood.

Searcher Detective Rick Wilson, since 1998 a Minnesota police chief, testified that during the search, he'd found a pair of shorts with blood on them on the floor, the shorts Brancaccio had worn at the crime scene.

Jan Simcsuk told of how on the evening of Friday, June 11, 1993, while driving west to east on Heatherwood Boulevard with her son Jesse in the car, she'd seen two people walking along the side of the road—an elderly woman and a young man. Looking back in her rearview mirror, she saw the young man making aggressive hand gestures. Asked to describe his face, she said it was "aggravated, agitated."

Mirman said, "How did the woman appear?"

"Fine."

"Was she turning to look at the man?"

"No, she was facing forward."

"Just to be clear, were they walking in the same direction you were driving?"

"Yes."

"Toward the berm?"

"Yes."

"Do you see this young man here in court? Could you point him out?"

She indicated the defendant. Shortly after, court recessed for the weekend.

Monday, January 11, day two of the trial. The friends of Victor Brancaccio took the stand, testifying for the state. Kristin Bonpartito, then seventeen, received a phone call from the defendant around 8:45 P.M., Friday, June 11, 1993, making plans for that night. Sounding out of breath, Brancaccio volunteered that, "I was out walking and I hit an old lady." He said it several times. Bonpartito didn't believe him. She drove to his house at around nine, and beeped the horn. Brancaccio came out. His mother followed, asking if he'd taken his medicine. He said he had. He got in and they drove to the house of another friend, Tina Pataritis. On the way, Brancaccio asked the witness to drive to the Heatherwood field, so he could get his Walkman, which he said he'd left there earlier, when he hit the old lady. She said no.

Mirman said, "On your way to Tina's house, did he say anything?"

Bonpartito said, "He put his hand on my shoulder and said I had to be his girlfriend. . . . I just brushed it off." They were at Tina's from nine-thirty to twelve-thirty, With her sister, hanging out, watching TV, eating pizza.

"Did you order pizza from the defendant's family's place?"

"No."

"During that time, did he make reference to the old lady?"

Bonpartito said, "He would get quiet sometimes and say that he hit an old lady and he was thinking about her. We all just thought it was a joke and trying to get attention."

"Were you kidding with him about beating up an old lady?"

"Yes."

"What would you say to him?"

"Don't get Victor mad, he might beat us up."

Mirman said, "During that evening, did you have skin lotion on or moisturizing lotion?"

"Yeah," Bonpartito said. "At one point, we were wrestling around and he said it smelled like the lady he had been with."

"Did he give you more details?"

"He said that he was walking down the street and that she told him to stop and that she would call the police if he didn't stop cursing." But later, in the car, he sat up and said, "You didn't believe me? Good, 'cause I just wanted to see what you thought." Bonpartito said she'd never seen the body and that Brancaccio had never asked her for any advice.

Roy Black established that throughout the evening, Brancaccio said that he'd hit an old lady, but that no one believed him. "He had mood swings that evening. You knew him for five years. Would you ever see mood swings where he'd get quiet and stare into space?"

Bonpartito said, "No."

"Before he went to the [Savannas] hospital, you never saw this?"

"No."

On redirect, the prosecution established that Brancaccio had never asked anyone to call the police, never said anything about getting help for the old lady. "There's an element of his personality that likes attention?"

Bonpartito said, "He would say things to be the center of attention."

"Before and after going to Savannas, how would you describe him?"

"The same Victor I had known both times."

Black on recross noted, "You said you can't always believe what Victor tells you? That's why you didn't listen that night?"

Bonpartito said, "Yes."

"He could make up stories?"

"Yes."

"Before he went to the mental hospital, you never saw him hurt old ladies?"

"No."

* * *

Next to testify was Tina Pataritis.

On Friday, June 11, at 9:30 P.M., Brancaccio and Kristin Bonpartito arrived at the house of Tina Pataritis, then twenty. Mirman said, "What did you three do?"

Pataritis said, "We were just going to watch TV, get pizza, hang."

"Did you order pizza? Where?"

"Big Apple."

"Is that owned by the defendant's parents?"

"No."

It is interesting to note that even after the murder, the defendant had been intent on ordering a non-Brancaccio pizza, the same infuriating preference that had sparked the argument with his mother.

Pataritis said that Brancaccio had brought up the subject of the old lady five or six times that night, about once every half hour, but she didn't believe him. "Throughout the whole night he would tell us, 'I think I hurt an old lady.' And then shrug it off with, 'I'm just kidding.'"

"Did he show you anything on his body that was supposedly related to the incident?"

"Yes. He said, 'Look at the blood on my arm.' And I'm like, where, Victor? And it looked like the blood from a mosquito bite smeared."

"Was he pointing it out to make you believe him?"

"I guess."

Brancaccio took a shower at her house, about fifteen minutes after arriving. He'd told Bonpartito earlier that he wanted to shower, but she told him there wasn't time before she picked him up. He hadn't showered since coming home from the field.

Roy Black's cross-examination stressed that no one at the house had believed Brancaccio's story about the old lady, even though he'd tried hard to make them believe. "He said, look at my arm because there's blood on it, to try to get you to believe it?"

Pataritis said, "Yes."

On Saturday, June 12, 1993, at 10:30 A.M., Angel Pellot, eighteen, was driving his car when Victor Brancaccio flagged him down for a ride to the family's Roma West bakery/pizzeria. Mirman said, "Did you have a conversation?"

Pellot said, "He said he had killed someone . . . he kept saying he killed an old lady. He said he did some wild shit last night." But the witness hadn't believed him. Brancaccio showed him the sneakers he was wearing. "They had blood all over them."

Brancaccio seemed unrepentant, bragging. After dropping off Brancaccio, Pellot later made contact with his buddy Jack Zaccheo, talking about the "murder." On June 13, Sunday night, they drove out to Heatherwood to look for a body to see if Brancaccio's story was true. The police pulled them over and detained them.

Jack Zaccheo took the stand. Now a husky, round-faced insurance agent, in June 1993 he'd been seventeen, in high school, working part-time at Roma West in St. Lucie West's busy Publix Plaza. At 10:45, Saturday morning, June 12, Zaccheo had been at work in the kitchen, washing dishes, when Brancaccio came up to him and said that he'd killed someone the night before. He seemed "normal . . . kind of casual, upbeat."

Zaccheo said, "In the morning when he first told me that he had killed someone, I remember him saying something about he went back to check on her. He told me that he thought that she was kind of grunting or something, like making a noise. He couldn't tell if she was actually breathing or not. And, uh, he asked her did she want some help and she didn't respond. I guess she was either unconscious or even dead, I don't know. And, uh, she did not respond to him so he just said, 'Well, fuck you then.' And then walked away."

But at that time, Zaccheo simply didn't believe Brancaccio, he said.

Zaccheo had gotten off work Saturday at 11:00 A.M., and was joined by Brancaccio who wanted to get some custom auto parts for his car. Zaccheo offered to help the boss's son go shopping for them. While driving Brancaccio home, they decided to go see the body. They went to Crabapple Cove, but saw a couple of phone trucks in the area and backed off, driving away. Zaccheo said, "I said, well, if it was there, they probably found it. . . . I felt if there was a body there, someone would have seen it."

They then picked up Lynette Winchester, Zaccheo's girlfriend. At eleven-thirty they stopped off at the house of Ivan Ortega. Ortega and his buddy Carlos Calle, worked for the Brancaccios. Ortega, Calle, Winchester, Zaccheo, and Brancaccio hung out. Brancaccio brought up the killing, but nobody gave it much of a play, just kidding around the edges of it, disbelieving.

Zaccheo, Winchester, and Brancaccio left to go shopping for auto parts, hitting a couple of stores, before going to McDonald's. Returning to Heatherwood to drop off Brancaccio, they noticed the phone trucks were gone and decided to make another try at seeing the body—if any.

While they were driving, Brancaccio told them a version of what had happened, saying that while he'd been walking on the main road of Heatherwood, "he encountered the lady and told us that she said something to him and then he got agitated and he struck her on the face and started beating her, dragged her to an opening in the berm. Behind there is where he finished beating her and kicking her. She said, 'You better stop or I'll call the police.' " Zaccheo said, "He didn't want her to be able to identify him. He said he was going to give her brain damage."

Park said, "Did he indicate if she tried to fight back?"

"She asked to stop and talk and he said, 'Fuck you.' "

Zaccheo drove back into the cul-de-sac and they saw the body.

Earlier, when they'd been talking at the restaurant, Zaccheo had said disbelievingly that Brancaccio couldn't just leave a body lying out there—what about fingerprints? "I kept saying, you know, 'What, you just left the body laying there? You know, you'll get caught if that's what you did.' Umm, well, he said, I'll just cover it up or I'll just run off to Italy or New York or something like that, he said. And, uh, he did say he was going to go back and cover up the fingerprints."

Park said, "Well, whose idea was it to cover up the fingerprints or use red spray paint?"

"That was his idea to use red spray paint."

"Did you ever suggest that to him?"

"Never."

"And whose idea was it to burn the body?"

"It was his."

"Did you ever suggest it to him?"

"No. 'Cause when he brought that up, I was thinking, where is he getting this stuff from—burning the body? And, uh, but I didn't say nothing. He said he was going to burn the body and I said, well, why would you do that? He said he was going to go back and cover up the prints."

Now that he knew there really was a body out in the field, a shook-up Zaccheo couldn't get rid of Brancaccio too soon. Brancaccio asked him for help in moving the body to a lake where he could dump it, suggesting that Zaccheo get the bakery van so they could use it for that purpose. Zaccheo said no and took Brancaccio home.

He said, "I kept thinking, I want him out of the car. . . . I didn't know what he was capable of doing—he mentioned burning the body."

Zaccheo had to go back to work, back to Roma West. He and Winchester were unsure of what to do. They thought about calling the police but they were scared. Zaccheo went to work, Winchester hanging out with him, keeping out of the way. She colored in some children's coloring books as a way to keep her mind off what she'd seen. Later, Victor Brancaccio met Zaccheo at the store, following him while he moved some items into the cooler. He told Zaccheo that he'd spray painted the corpse.

Perhaps sensing Zaccheo's newfound reserve, the next day, Sunday, Brancaccio asked him, "What, are you not my friend anymore?" Zaccheo was none too eager to spend time with Brancaccio. He and Winchester had discussed telling the police, but worried, "What if they don't know it's Victor? Then he'll come after us."

Lynette Winchester was over at her brother Larry's house. After working a split shift, Zaccheo got off at 10 P.M., going to Ortega's house. Angel Pellot was there, he wanted to get something to eat. Zaccheo left his car and rode with Pellot. They got to talking about Brancaccio, Pellot saying, "He told me he killed someone. . . . Did they catch him?" They went to see, and the cops stopped them.

Park said, "Do you see the person in this court-room that told you that he hit this woman?"

"Yes, I do," Zaccheo said, pointing to Brancac-cio.

The prosecutor had Zaccheo repeat some of Brancaccio's choice remarks, getting them into the record. Zaccheo said, "He said she was so knocked out, he could have fucked her."

Park said, "Did you ask him, 'Don't you feel bad?' "

"He said, 'I don't have a heart. . . .' "

"Did you suggest any way to remove the body or cover it up?"

"No, I told him he was going to get caught."

Roy Black maintained that what was described by prosecutors as Brancaccio's "cover-up" was ac-tually inspired by his "friends," then carried out by the suggestible, borderline defendant. Starting his cross, he established that at the time of the murder, Zaccheo had been two years older than Brancaccio, that Brancaccio had looked up to him, and implied he'd had been looking for ad-vice from Zaccheo when he'd approached him Saturday, June 12, at Roma West.

Black said, "You told him there was a problem about fingerprints?"

Zaccheo said, "I had mentioned, 'What are you

going to do, just leave the body? You'll get caught.' "

"You were the first to mention fingerprints? Victor didn't say anything about fingerprints?"

"Yes."

"You said, 'How could you leave a body out there with fingerprints?' "

Zaccheo said that he was just talking, that he hadn't believed that Brancaccio had killed anyone. "If I had believed him, I wouldn't have had that conversation."

When Brancaccio showed Zaccheo his blood-stained sneakers, hadn't Zaccheo said, "You better throw them away"? Zaccheo said he didn't remember saying that. When Brancaccio had talked of burning the body, hadn't Zaccheo told him not to do it because the firetrucks would come? Yes, Zaccheo said. Brancaccio had then asked him what would be good to burn the body with, what was flammable, and Zaccheo said, any number of things? "Yes."

Black said, "Did you have a conversation in which it was discussed that spray paint was flammable?"

Zaccheo said, "No."

"You deny that?"

"Yeah."

"Did he tell you he tried to burn the body with Vaseline?"

One theory was that Brancaccio had some half-baked notion that Vaseline was flammable, and that he'd actually tried to use it as a fire accelerant on the corpse. Another theory held that he was just confabulating and hadn't made the attempt.

"He told me that. He said it didn't work and that's when he spray painted the body," Zaccheo said.

Black expressed incredulity about Zaccheo's earlier statement that he'd played baseball on Sunday, wondering how he could have been so unaffected by seeing the body that he was able to play. Zaccheo said, by way of refuting the charge of callous indifference, "I struck out. It did bother me."

The defense tried to paint Zaccheo as a false friend, a user and manipulator. Black pointed out that on Saturday, after working at the pizzeria, when they'd gone to three auto parts stores, Brancaccio had loaned the witness money to buy a set of items. "You said that you would pay him back?"

Zaccheo said, "Yes, sir, but he went to jail."

"You didn't return the money?"

"I couldn't. . . . I wanted to give it back to him, but I'm not going to go to his house and say, 'Hi, I'm Jack, here's the money. . . .' "

Black returned to Saturday at the store, when Brancaccio had approached Zaccheo, who was washing dishes. "He walked right up and said, 'Last night I killed somebody,' right out of the blue?"

Zaccheo said, "Yeah, out of the blue."

"Did you have a feeling that he looked up to you, wanted to be friends?"

"Yeah."

"He was looking for advice, wanted something?"

"I don't know, I can't answer that. . . ."

"Reaching out for help?"

"I don't know."

"But certainly one interpretation could be that he was seeking advice?"

"Could be."

Black said that Zaccheo had never provided the help that Brancaccio needed, never told him they had to call the police. Zaccheo said he didn't believe Brancaccio. Black countered that he hadn't suggested contacting the police after he'd seen the body, either. "In fact, you said, 'Victor, you are crazy, you killed somebody right in front of your house.'"

Zaccheo said, "Yes, I did say that." He'd told Brancaccio that he would get in trouble, and that Brancaccio had said he would go to New York or Italy. "I said, 'You'll get caught; the cops ain't stupid. . . .'" He told Brancaccio he'd go to jail, reminding him that Florida has the death penalty. Brancaccio said, "Yeah, they'll probably give me the chair."

Black said, "Isn't it true he didn't do anything until you started giving him advice?"

Zaccheo said, "I didn't give him any advice."

"You knew he was taking medication. You knew he had been in the hospital for a while. Did you ever think that here is somebody who has a mental problem, perhaps I ought to do something?"

"I didn't know he had a mental problem and I didn't take any steps."

Prosecutor Lynn Park called Lynette Winchester. Now twenty-two, in June 1993 she was seventeen, out of school, working at Taco Bell, and living with her older brother, Larry Winchester, in Port St. Lucie. She was Jack Zaccheo's girlfriend and knew Victor Brancaccio from school. On Saturday, June 11, at about 11:30 A.M., she'd been at Ivan Ortega's house, when she heard something about somebody killing someone. It was all vague, loose talk and she didn't believe it. Later, she, Zaccheo and Brancaccio went out to shop for auto parts.

Park said, "While you were driving around, did Victor say anything about an old lady?"

Winchester said, "He said he killed her. . . . He hit her in the face, then put her in a headlock, dragged her to the hill, and continued to beat her." But she said she hadn't believed him, not even when Brancaccio showed her what looked like blood on his sneakers.

Later, when they were taking him home, Brancaccio directed them to the field and showed them the body. Winchester didn't get too close, but was close enough to see that the body was wearing blue shorts and was not painted red at this time. She asked Brancaccio why he'd done it, and he said it was because the old lady had been "talking shit."

After they dropped Brancaccio off at his home, why didn't she and Zaccheo contact the police?

Winchester said, "We were scared of his family." They were also scared that somehow they'd be blamed for the crime.

Later, she tagged along when Zaccheo went to work at 7 P.M. at Roma West on the second half of his split shift, delivering pizza. She hung out with him, helping with deliveries. Brancaccio was there and told them he'd tried to burn the body, but it hadn't worked, so he'd spray painted it.

What was Brancaccio's demeanor while telling her this? Did he show any remorse?

"No," Winchester said.

On Sunday, June 13, she worked from eight to four at Taco Bell, seeing neither Zaccheo nor Brancaccio. At about nine P.M., talking to her older brother, Larry Winchester, on the phone, she told him, "Jack's friend killed a lady." He didn't believe her at first, but he came over, accompanied by his girlfriend and her baby. All four got in the car and the witness directed them to the body. After Larry Winchester saw it, he went straight to the police.

Park said, "When you saw the body again, did it look different than before?"

Winchester said, "Yes. It was spray painted red."

"Did Victor tell you why he left the body there?"

"It was too heavy to move." Brancaccio had also said that Frazier "was strong for an old bitch."

Roy Black's cross focused on what Zaccheo had said to Brancaccio on Saturday. "Jack asked about what Victor had done with the sneakers. Jack told Victor to throw the sneakers away because they were evidence."

She said, "I remember Jack telling him to throw them away, but I don't know why."

"Jack said, 'You're crazy, you're going to get caught, throw the sneakers away.' Isn't it a fact that he told Victor to throw them away because they had blood on them?"

"Yes."

"It's fair to say that Jack was giving advice to Victor about what to do with the evidence," said Black.

"Yes."

"Jack's a take-charge kind of guy."

"Right."

Black said that Brancaccio had never told her and Zaccheo about not calling the police. "Did he ever tell you not to call the police, please don't call the police?"

She said, "No."

"You didn't want to call the police."

"We were scared of the Brancaccio family."

"You were too scared to make a call because of the Brancaccio family, but you spent the night [Saturday] at the pizzeria," said Black.

"Nobody knew anything so we weren't scared

to stay at the pizzeria," Winchester said. "I had nowhere else to go."

Port St. Lucie Police Department Detective Sergeant Scott Beck had interviewed Victor Brancaccio on the morning of the arrest, getting his taped confession. Beck testified that Brancaccio had been properly given his Miranda rights and had read and signed a Port St. Lucie Police Department rights waiver form, which was now admitted into evidence. No threats or promises were made to the defendant.

Lawrence Mirman said, "You are not required to notify the defendant's parents prior to interrogation?"

Beck said, "No." His understanding of the law was that once a "child" is taken into custody, the parents are contacted in order to know where the child is—which had been done in the Brancaccio case. Beck's tape of Brancaccio's confession was admitted into evidence over defense objections that it should be inadmissable because police had "lied" about trying to contact the defendant's parents.

Beck told of his Sunday night interview of a reluctant Jack Zaccheo. "At first, he was apprehensive, he did not want to be involved. He was not cooperative. I told him we knew he had first-hand knowledge and if he would not be a witness, he would be a suspect."

The defense was eager to question Beck, but

passed at this time, reserving their cross-examination for later, when Beck would be returning to the stand.

The state called Janice Taylor, the expert criminalist who'd done the microanalysis of a paint chip found on a Hog Trail Murder victim. Taylor testified that the red paint coating Mollie Frazier's body was consistent with paint from the spray paint cans found by investigators in Brancaccio's house.

District Medical Examiner Dr. Frederick Hobin had done over four hundred autopsies a year for eleven years, and had testified over one hundred times as a medical expert. He found that Mollie Frazier had died due to blunt trauma. Repeated blows to the skull inflicted crushing lacerations that came not from a fist, but from some blunt object.

The chest had suffered tremendous damage; the right side of the chest was crushed, ribs were fractured. Hobin said, "It would have taken tremendous force. This is not just a trivial impact."

He offered his scenario of the attack. "I have a concept of what might have happened. It would be my opinion. I wasn't there. . . .

"Mrs. Frazier was battered by another person. They were in a face-to-face position. The other person battered her about the face and head. The first battering was with a blunt instrument. In order to protect herself, Mrs. Frazier ducked her head and raised her hands to protect her face. She received impact injuries to the top of the head and arm and left hand. As a result, she might have fallen backwards and been on the ground. And with her back braced against the ground, another person may have continued the attack as she was down and came down on her forcefully with knees on her chest, compressing the chest against the ground . . . and the heavy weight crushed her chest and broke ribs and perhaps she might have suffered some additional injuries to the head as the battering continued."

Mirman said, "What would be the course of events leading to her death?"

"Forceful blows could cause her brain to cease functioning; the crushing force to her chest would cause her respiration to cease. She would die in a matter of minutes." The medical examiner testified he found no evidence of sexual assault on the body.

Schulz's cross began late in Tuesday's session, continuing over to Wednesday, January 13, the third day of the trial. Schulz suggested that a blow to the head had triggered a heart attack that caused Mollie Frazier's death. Hobin agreed it was possible.

Schulz said, "You talked about a kicking injury."

"It's possible she was kicked on the ground."

"What do you look for, to tell the differences between a kick and a stomping?"

"Footwear marks."

"The first blow to her head could have caused her death?"

"Yes." Hobin admitted that his interpretation of events was not the only one. Schulz tried to underline the defense proposition that Brancaccio had killed Mollie Frazier in a frenzy. "It was a quick assault and death? It was consistent with a rapid outburst?"

Hobin said, "Yes . . . I thought that a quick violent assault was more likely than any other possibility."

Forensic scientist Dan Nippes had a quarter-century's expertise. He testified that the strand of hair adhering to a piece of the plastic gun was consistent with that of Mollie Frazier's.

The prosecution recalled Detective Scott Beck, who said that Brancaccio's demeanor during his statement of Monday, June 14, was "commonplace, calm, not agitated, not anything out of the ordinary."

The tape of Brancaccio's interview was then played in court. It opened with Brancaccio saying that he understood his rights and was willing to answer questions without his attorney being present. Beck said, "I understand you had an argument and that led to something you didn't want to happen."

Brancaccio said, "What are you talking about?"

"The old lady."

"The old lady?"

"Yes, Victor, I know."

"What're you talking about?"

"First-degree murder."

"I swear to God I didn't murder!"

"Don't swear to God."

"I promise I didn't murder!"

"Don't swear."

"What can I tell you to make you believe me?"

"Nothing, because I know what you did." Beck then told Brancaccio he had a witness who saw him. "Victor, what you did was serious."

Brancaccio said, "I didn't do it."

"What didn't you do?"

"What you were talking about. . . . I'm not that kind of kid; my mom would tell you."

Beck said that the spray paint Brancaccio used to hide his fingerprints on the body may have instead enhanced them, bringing them out.

Brancaccio said that he was walking and the lady said something to him and he told her to shut up. She said he was low class in a high-class neighborhood, so he just hit her. "I was scared after that. I didn't know if I should help her or continue what I was doing."

"What did you do?"

"Continue what I was doing." Brancaccio then started crying. Beck asked if he put the lady in a headlock. Brancaccio said he just dragged her by the arm. "Next day, she was still breathing. I asked if she wanted help. She wouldn't answer, but she was still breathing. I asked if she wanted me to call an ambulance, she didn't answer. I got scared."

"What did you hit her with?"

"A Walkman and a fake gun." Brancaccio said that he was carrying a replica toy gun. "I said stop or I will beat the shit out of her and then I punched her. . . . She looked at me and said, 'I never thought you would be this kind of person.' "

Brancaccio told of returning to burn the body. It wouldn't burn, so he spray painted her instead. "I thought it would destroy fingerprints."

"What did you do next, after you spray painted her?"

"I went home and cried. . . . I never thought I would be like this. I never thought I would kill anyone, never thought this would happen."

Beck said, "Did you do anything sexual to this woman?"

Brancaccio said, "Absolutely not."

"When it was happening, did you know it was wrong?"

"While I was doing it, I didn't know. . . . The next day I knew I did something wrong. . . . I didn't know if I should tell someone or let her stay there. I didn't know where to start."

Brancaccio said that when the old lady "was yelling at me, she called me a little bastard. I said, that's not my name, my name is Victor. She kept on lecturing me and I got tired of it—telling me what kind of music to listen to . . . I was listening to Dr. Dre."

When Brancaccio finished telling his story, Beck said, "Victor, I'm proud of you."

"I hope I don't get into trouble."

"You did the right thing."

"I know I did a bad thing."

"You understand you'll be arrested?"

"Yes."

"Any further questions?"

"My mom is going to be notified?"

"Yes."

"My mom is a nervous woman; she might pass away—she gets sick easy. Tell my dad first."

Beck asked, after Brancaccio hit the lady, did he feel he had to kill her?

"Not kill her, but hurt her pretty bad."

The tape ended.

On Thursday, January 14, day four, the defense put Beck on the stand for Black's cross-examination, counsel alleging that Beck and other investigators had worked together to "isolate" Brancaccio. "You didn't want Victor's parents to be present at the questioning?"

Beck said, "I never really thought about it."

Brancaccio had asked if his parents had been notified and was told that it was being taken care of. "That is a lie?"

"No."

Black continued. "Victor has told you by this time that sometimes he has weird feelings. You know he's sixteen, under medication. . . . You ask him, 'When this was happening, did you know what you were doing was wrong?' He told you, 'I

didn't know it was wrong while I was doing it.'
There was conversation about whether Victor felt
remorse. . . . He tells you he felt bad for her?"

Beck said, "Yes, sir."

"He says he went home and he was shaking?"

"Yes, sir."

"He says when he was at home he was scared,
he didn't know what to do?"

"Yes, sir."

"He says, 'I never thought I was going to be
like this'? He tells you, 'I had tears in my eyes'?"

"Yes, sir."

Black asked how the family had learned the
news. Beck said that a female police lieutenant
called the house to tell the parents. "I remember
her telling somebody, 'Victor just confessed,' and
I heard a voice in the background screaming,
'No, no.' "

Having called its final witness, the state rested.

The defense began presenting its case, calling
its first expert witness, forensic neuropsychologist
Dr. Antoinette Appel, who'd researched the case
of Victor Brancaccio. She said the defendant's
premature birth and near-drowning incident as a
toddler had given him a brain injury. His academic record was "horrible. He failed first grade.
In second grade he was in special ed. . . . He
goes through grades with large numbers of Ds,
then switches to another school."

Brancaccio was borderline mentally retarded,

she said. He'd taken his first drink at age fifteen and had been using alcohol for a year before the April 16, 1993, incident, where he was caught stealing a six-pack of beer. Appel said he was admitted to the hospital because "he was hostile, he had run away, he had burned himself with cigarettes, he was drinking and drugging himself to the point of suicidal threats."

The most important feature of his Savannas Hospital stay was the difference in behavior before he was administered the antidepressant drug Zoloft and after, Appel said. Before Zoloft, his affect (facial expression) was flat—he was listless, depressed, and felt bad about himself.

Black said, "And what happens after he starts on the Zoloft?"

Appel said, "He's rude. He's snappy. He has poor concentration, difficulty sitting still, he becomes quick to anger, he is rude, hyper-verbal. . . . He goes from being flat, not really giving you a lot of trouble, to being hyper, angry, loud, verbose, and giving folks trouble.

"At the end, he still says that he's sick. 'I'm afraid, I'm afraid of relapsing, I'm not in control. I don't feel good. Don't make me go home.' "

"From your examination of the records, are you able to determine why he was discharged from the hospital on May 11, 1993?"

"Yes, I am able to determine why he was discharged from the hospital on May eleventh. And that is because his insurance ran out."

Appel said she saw Brancaccio on July 1, 1998.

"He is brain damaged; he is depressed, and in my opinion, he had an adverse depression from Zoloft. He basically said of the medication that he feels bad on it, it doesn't make him feel good."

"Doctor, do you have an opinion whether or not at the time of the assault on Mrs. Frazier . . . Victor Brancaccio met the standards of criminal responsibility under Florida law?"

"At that instant in time he didn't know the difference between right or wrong. He was [in] involuntary intoxication; he couldn't appreciate what he was doing. He didn't know at the instant that his behaviors were wrong. I don't think he could form an intent. I don't think he could think that well. I think his brain is sufficiently disorganized and his behavior sufficiently disorganized that he can't think that well."

Black said, "How would you describe his actions, from what you've read or heard, the actions that happened during the assault?"

"A frenzy," Appel said.

"What do you mean by a 'frenzy'?"

"An uncontrolled event that plays itself out. I was trying to think of a good analogy as you asked the question. On the Fourth of July, throwing a match onto a barge of firecrackers. All right? It's going to continue to go off until it burns itself out. And when it burns itself out, it'll stop. And there's not a whole lot you can do in between. It's a frenzy. It's just totally out of proportion."

On cross, prosecutor Lynn Park addressed the question of whether Zoloft had caused Brancaccio's aggressiveness, pointing out that the October 1992 fight incident, the April 1993 theft of the beer, and Brancaccio's statement that he wanted to kill his brother had all occurred prior to his taking Zoloft.

Asked if she thought the defendant was insane, Appel said, "That is my opinion."

"He didn't know what he was doing?"

"I think that is true. I think he has brain damage. . . . Surely the Zoloft had a major impact. I think he had depression and substance-abuse problems and brain damage. . . . I think that he is pushed over the brink by Zoloft. Zoloft is not a bad drug. It's just a bad drug for him."

"For him alone?"

"No. A large percentage have to come off because of side-effects."

On Friday, January 15, the fifth day, another defense expert witness, Dr. John Smilak, said it was his opinion that the blows to the head could have given Mollie Frazier a heart attack, causing her death. On cross, he agreed with the prosecution's contention that Frazier's chest injuries were equivalent to those sustained in an automobile crash, and that she was still alive when the crushing occurred. He believed that she'd probably survived the blows to her head for a few minutes; then her eighty-one-year-old body gave out and she died.

Forensic psychologist Dr. Ronald Schlensky felt

that because of Victor Brancaccio's near-drowning incident at age two, "his brain was deprived—the result is that he has to operate with limited or compromised capacity." Brancaccio was "a reduced human person, a borderline retarded human being. He has limited intellectual resources. . . . He is able to operate socially, though. He does not come across as a retarded person, but rather as a reduced person."

Black said, "How many patients have you treated with the drug Zoloft?"

"Just an estimate, I'd say hundreds."

"Are there side effects associated to the use of Zoloft?"

"The potential side effects are myriad, so to speak. That is, one can develop a Parkinson–like state of restlessness and impaired motor ability. One can become psychotic; one can become agitated. So, there's a small subset of patients that get much worse as a result of taking the medicine. They get irritable, they get restless, their personality can change, they can become psychotic. And so, again, this has to be recognized and managed properly."

Black said, "In this particular case, have you, based upon the study of the records and your clinical interview of Victor Brancaccio, come to a conclusion about his ability to form the intent to commit a crime at the time of the assault on Mrs. Frazier?"

Schlensky said, "He did not at the time he committed this offense have the mental capacity to recognize what he was doing, to be able to appreciate it, to understand the consequences or to control himself."

"Why do you say that?"

"Because he had regressed at that time to a psychotic state." The administration of Zoloft had pushed him over the brink.

Lynn Park's cross was tough. "You say he was a compromised person? What made him leave his home and beat a woman to death?"

Schlensky began, "I'm going to give you a careful answer to that question. First, I want to start with explaining what it means to have a damaged brain—"

"Was it your opinion that because he was taking Zoloft and he was a compromised person, he killed this person?"

"That's a complicated question," the witness said.

"Was Brancaccio insane at the time of the murder?"

"That's a legal term. I'm a medical doctor. That's for the court to decide. I can tell you if he had a mental disorder."

"Did his mental abilities prevent him from knowing right from wrong?"

"Yes."

Park pressed. "When do you think he became someone who did not know right from wrong?"

Schlensky gave his interpretation of the events leading to the murder. "Victor felt suicidal, he's just been in the hospital, he's just had an argument with his mother. He left that incident feeling as though he was a worthless human."

Park said, "At that point he knew right from wrong?"

"Yes . . . but unfortunately there were other events that transpired. He flipped out and behaved like a raging beast, functioning at the level of an animal. It's a short circuit."

"When he was walking down the street, he knew right from wrong?"

"Yes."

"When he hit Mrs. Frazier?"

"No."

"When he left the house carrying the gun? Do you know if he left the house with a plastic gun?"

Schlensky admitted he didn't know. "I didn't discuss it with him."

"Did he know right from wrong when he kept hitting her?"

"He was out of touch with reality. He suddenly became acutely psychotic."

Park, disbelieving, said, "He knows right from wrong when he leaves the house and he's rapping to music and then he meets Frazier and becomes psychotic?"

"Kind of."

"After beating her, does he know right from wrong?"

"I think he emerged from the psychotic state and questions what happened. . . . He's thinking, what happened here? There are features of his conduct that are bizarre and regressed."

"When he went home and lied to his mother, did he know right from wrong?"

"I think so," Schlensky said. "There was a beginning and an end. The killing happened during the period when he was most regressed."

"When you talked to him in September, did he know right from wrong? He knew the nature of his actions?"

"Yes."

After Schlensky, the defense rested. Court recessed for the weekend.

Monday was a holiday and trial resumed on Tuesday, January 19, as the state presented its rebuttal witnesses. Dr. Darryl Matthews, a psychiatrist, testified for the prosecution regarding possible side effects from Zoloft. In premarketing studies, a certain statistical minority, about one in a hundred, had suffered adverse reactions to the drug.

The regular physical disorders associated with it were yawning and male sexual dysfunction. Reported but infrequently occurring disorders included depression, amnesia, apathy, abnormal dreams, hallucinations, delusion. Rare disorders were increased libido and illusion. Again, rates of aggression in controlled studies were one in a hundred.

"It means it's something to keep in the back of your mind," Matthews said. "Aggression is common in society. It may be more common in people who are likely to receive Zoloft. That's not surprising, and not cause to conclude that it's caused by the drug." Surveys of the population indicate that "about two percent of the population will say, 'Yes, I've done something violent.'"

Asked about the relationship between Zoloft and violence, Matthews said, "My opinion is based on experience and the [scientific] literature. There is no known causal relationship between Zoloft and violence."

Mirman said, "Does Zoloft cause aggressive behavior?"

"Zoloft is effective in treating aggressiveness."

"It's used to curb aggression?"

"Yes, it's recommended."

Wasn't it important to look at the defendant's behavior prior to Zoloft? "Yes, you couldn't say it was caused by Zoloft if they were there anyway," Matthews said. Brancaccio had been violent to his parents before taking the drug, with one of the examining doctors noting that Brancaccio said he had pushed his mother on several occasions. In the hospital, she'd said, "I feel like a punching bag sometimes."

The witness said the October 1992 fight incident was important because "it's an example of violence with no Zoloft. The best predictor of future violence is past violence." Brancaccio's school records showed he was involved in many disciplinary incidents. Brancaccio had reported that since age thirteen or fourteen, he'd had nightmares about killing people.

As for the defense claims that Brancaccio's affect and behavior had changed from depressed to hyperactive following the administration of Zoloft, Matthews went to the record. When Brancaccio was admitted to Savannas Hospital on April 19, the admission notes stated that the patient exhibited "impulsivity, alcohol abuse, irritable, potential for violence, depression." The next day's notes described him as "angry." On the twenty-fourth, there was a notation about his "poor anger management." On the twenty-sixth, he was "sarcastic."

On April 27, during a meeting between staffers and his parents, Brancaccio became agitated. This was the same meeting during which Lina Brancaccio said that sometimes she felt like a punching bag. Matthews said, "What this told me is that he became agitated involving relationships with his parents. The agitation . . . comes from life events. He can't yet identify what are the things that cause anger."

All this happened before he started taking Zoloft. An evaluation made by a psychologist before the Zoloft was started described Brancaccio's "very unusual hyperactivity level."

After Brancaccio was on Zoloft, on May 3, he denied having any side effects. On May 5, Brancaccio played the role of "class clown." But rather than attributing that to the drug, Matthews ascribed it to the defendant's anxiety about being released from the hospital, "the thought of discharge, going back to a situation that has some risks." On May 9, earlier in the day, Brancaccio was described as talkative and joking with the staff, but his demeanor changed when his mother showed up for a visit, when, according to staffers' notes, he became "rude and snappy."

Mirman said, "That's part of the problem, relationships causing anxiety?"

Matthews said, "I think that there is a problem with how he's relating to parents. . . . I think he's concerned that some problems with the relationship may come up again."

Brancaccio, uneasy about his release from the hospital, became hyperverbal, testing the limits. "He was expressing fear of discharge, testing the limits, not dealing well with leaving the hospital. There was some anxious acting out, to take the focus off the discharge. He was angry, but he processed his behavior, admitted to being fearful," Matthews said.

Mirman noted Brancaccio's remarks about being "afraid of going back to my old ways." The witness said that meant Brancaccio's old ways of drinking and being aggressive. Notes made by Savannas doctors treating Brancaccio after his release on an outpatient basis recorded that he was taking his medication and experiencing no side effects.

After Brancaccio was arrested and put in jail, he was taken off Zoloft in March of 1994. Mirman said, "Specifically going to June of 1994, when the defendant was not on the drug Zoloft, did you see any notation there that was significant to you regarding whether Zoloft had an aggressive effect on the defendant?"

Matthews said, "There's a jail note that involves some pretty serious thoughts of aggression. He says he wants to go and kill other inmates. Later says, 'He's been getting increased urges to kill. Told his father on the phone that he's been getting urges to kill his parents and lawyer. Says he wants to feel the high of killing.' " All this after he was off Zoloft.

On cross, Roy Black addressed Brancaccio's jailhouse behavior, arguing that his aggressive thoughts were a response to being in a violent environment. "Victor was assaulted in jail. On September 20, he reported inmates took his food and threatened him. . . . In July 1993, he was found with swellings and abrasions, he had a bump on his head the size of a quarter." In January 1994, doctors had to put staples in his head to close a wound. He reported in February that some older boys tried to sodomize him. Black said, "It certainly appears that he was being abused in the jail, does it not?"

Matthews said, "Abused or fighting, certainly yes."

"If you were in jail, you're sixteen years old, people are throwing feces at you, beating you up, and trying to sodomize you, it wouldn't be unusual at all to hate those people, would it?"

"You would certainly hate them," Matthews conceded.

Black said that on September 21, 1993, Brancaccio reported hearing the voice of an old lady. While in jail, he was put on Haldol, a potent psychiatric drug, for five months. In October, he reported hearing women's voices saying they were going to get him. On October 31—Halloween— he said he was hearing "scary things." In November, he said he felt like he was going crazy. In March 1994, he said he was having a breakdown. He heard voices of women, some saying he was going to be killed. In August 1994, he suffered from depression. In November 1994, he was overheard crying. When asked what was wrong, he said that he did not want to hurt anyone, and also said, "Help me. I need help."

Black said that some people do report experiencing adverse effects from Zoloft, such as auditory hallucinations, aggressiveness, manifestations of psychiatric disorders, and the inability to function and meet reality. "Not everyone reacts the same to medication."

Matthews said, "Correct."

"It could work on ninety-nine percent, but be fatal to one percent. Some people can die from side effects."

"Yes."

"Brains react differently. People with brain damage might react differently."

"They may."

"Was Zoloft tested on people with brain damage?"

"Not specifically." The witness agreed that possible side effects of Zoloft include hyperactivity, irritability, and paranoia.

Black turned to Brancaccio's having been prescribed the powerful drug Haldol for five months while in prison. "Wasn't he put on Haldol because of auditory hallucinations?"

Matthews said, "I don't know if he was really having them."

"Is there a way to figure out whether people are malingering or not?"

"The record in this case is so full of faking and malingering, it's never clear if he is really having that kind of symptom."

Black said the clinician who'd prescribed Haldol for Brancaccio had decided he had hallucinations. Matthews called that decision "mistaken," saying that the jail psychiatrist agreed Brancaccio didn't need it.

A Savannas Hospital doctor had raised the possibility that Brancaccio suffered from some sort of organic brain damage. Another report found that he was "susceptible to influence and manipulation." Black said, "He's the type that's susceptible?"

"That's what it says."

"People suggest he do things, and he might do them?"

"That's consistent with the finding."

Black cited other reports on Brancaccio, " 'He was very immature . . . attitudes simplistic and naïve, more characteristic of those expected in a younger child . . . lack of self-awareness, impressionable. . . .'

"When you see youngsters who have low I.Q. and are learning disabled, you would look for birth injury as a possible explanation?"

Matthews said, "Yes."

The defense had no further questions. On redirect, Mirman asked about an evaluation made of Brancaccio at Savannas before he went on Zoloft "that showed a likelihood of future asocial behavior. What does asocial mean?"

Matthews said, "Probably delinquent, antisocial." The report said Brancaccio had conduct disorder, which the witness defined as "a repetitive pattern of behavior in which the rights of others or the norms of society are violated, a pattern of rule violation."

In Savannas, Brancaccio had undergone an MRI test. Mirman said, "What is an MRI?"

"A brain-imaging technique that can determine whether there are abnormalities in the brain. This test didn't show any," Mirman said.

Mirman focused on Brancaccio's jailhouse claims of auditory hallucinations, "hearing voices." He said, "In regard to the defendant's self-reports of hallucinations, first of all, when someone is charged with murder and claims hallucination, do you check that out and how?"

Matthews said, "When someone accused of a crime says 'hallucination,' you have to suspect this is being made up. There are a range of observations used to detect malingering. Some were done by Dr. Martell. He says the patient has malingered. Doctors who have seen him have found he makes up symptoms. He himself admitted as much."

"What does 'malingering' mean?"

"Falsifying symptoms."

"Do you think he hallucinated?"

"I have to be very skeptical. There were tests used to determine the issue."

"What was the outcome?"

"The determination was that Victor malingered."

State's expert witness Dr. Greg Landrum had performed the court-ordered psychological examination of Brancaccio to determine if he was competent to stand trial. He testified that he found no evidence that the defendant suffered from hallucinations. His report had said of Brancaccio, "Although moderately caring and responsive, he is not notably compassionate."

Lynn Park said, "What is your opinion as to Brancaccio's mental state at the time of the murder?"

Landrum said, "I feel he was able to establish right from wrong and establish intentional thought."

"He was able to form intent?"

"Yes."

"What was it he said that led to the conclusion he was able to form the intent to commit crimes?"

Landrum said it was the moment after Bran-

On August 15, 1994, Stanley Burden, 24, claimed a man named Dan had tied him up and tried to strangle him in the Hog Trails.

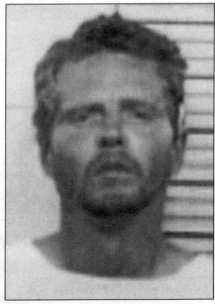

Convicted of stealing Daniel Conahan, Sr.'s car, David Payton's story about posing for nude pictures while tied to a tree wasn't believed.

REWARD

IDENTITIES BEING SOUGHT

JOHN DOE #1
JOHN DOE #2

(ACTUAL LIKENESS MAY BE DIFFERENT)

WHITE MALE, APPROXIMATELY 25 TO 35 YEARS OLD, 5' 9" TALL, 150 TO 160 POUNDS, BROWN HAIR. DISCOVERED 02/01/94 IN NORTHERN CHARLOTTE COUNTY.

WHITE MALE, APPROXIMATELY 35 TO 45 YEARS OLD, APPROXIMATELY 6' OR TALLER, HEAVY OR MUSCULAR BUILD, BROWN HAIR. DISCOVERED IN NORTH PORT OFF OF PLAMEDON ROAD.

THE REMAINS OF JOHN DOE #1 AND #2 WERE RECOVERED FROM WOODED AREAS. ANYONE HAVING INFORMATION CONCERNING THE IDENTITY OF EITHER OF THESE TWO SUBJECTS SHOULD CONTACT THE HOMICIDE TASK FORCE AT (941) 764-1598 OR THE CRIME STOP LINE AT 1 (800) 780-TIPS (8477).

Missing persons flyer for John Doe #1 and #2 (the two men found mutilated in the Hog Trails between 1994 and 1996).

John Doe #3, found in March 1996, was identified through fingerprints three years later as William John Melaragno, Jr.

Victim Richard Montgomery, 21, was found on April 16, 1996.

Victim Kenny Lee Smith's skull was found under Montgomery's body. Smith had been cut to pieces with a handsaw.

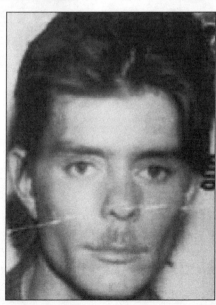

Aerial shot of the Hog Trails.

Daniel Conahan, Jr., 42, was
arrested for killing Montgomery.

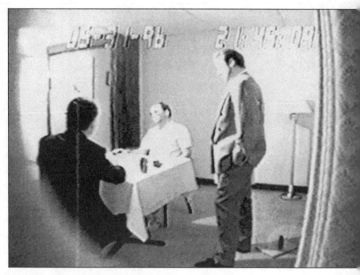

Police questioned Conahan about all the murdered men.

Bank video of Conahan helped establish his
whereabouts on the day of Montgomery's murder.

Conahan (*left*) hears the verdict of guilty.

Victim Mollie Mae Frazier, 81.

Frazier's body had been spray-painted red and set on fire.

Victor Brancaccio, 16, was arrested after bragging to friends that he'd killed an "old lady."

Brancaccio beat Frazier with a plastic toy gun.

Brancaccio showed Tina Panarities the blood on his arm.

Jack Zaccheo testified that Brancaccio showed him the body.

District Medical Examiner Dr. Frederick Hoban testified that repeated blows to the head with a blunt object caused Frazier's death.

Brancaccio (*left*) and his attorneys waiting for the verdict.

Eugene and Adelina Brancaccio, the defendant's parents.

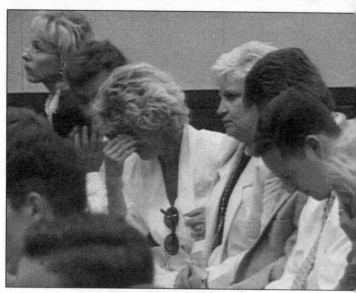

The Brancaccio family reacts to the
verdict of guilty of first degree murder.

Brancaccio is fingerprinted after
being sentenced to life in prison.

Victims Joseph and Barbara Stocks.

Victim Heather Stocks, 18, is remembered on her tombstone.

The Stocks and their daughter were found shot to death in their kitchen.

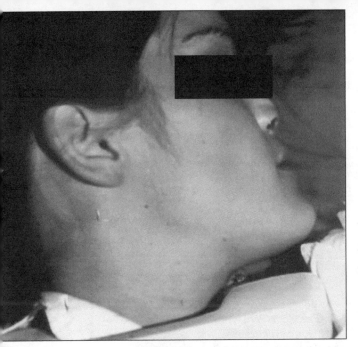

Heather Stocks was brutally shot to death.

Eagle Scout Heath Stocks, 20, received three life sentences for killing his family.

Assistant Scoutmaster Charles "Jack" Walls III, 51, was convicted of raping Heath Stocks and five other boy scouts.

Walls being escorted outside after being sentenced to four life terms plus eighty years.

caccio punched Frazier, "the moment of pause" during which he decided what to do with her and then took her over the berm.

"Did the defendant know what he was doing at the time he murdered Mollie Frazier?"

"Yes, he did," Landrum said.

"Did he know what he was doing when he lied to his mother?"

"Yes, he did."

"He was competent to stand trial?"

"Yes."

"Knows right from wrong?"

"Yes."

"At any time, did you find him to be psychotic or delusional?"

"No."

Landrum had seen Brancaccio on November 10, 1993, at the jail's medical wing.

On cross, Black asked if his then sixteen-year-old client was shorter than most young men his age. Landrum said he'd have to agree. Black said, "Wasn't he smaller than almost all the inmates in jail?"

The witness demurred. "He did not appear so significantly smaller than others that it struck a chord with me."

"At St. Lucie jail, there's a lot of tough people? It's not a place one would want to be?"

"I would agree with that."

Black said that inmates had been terrorizing Brancaccio, that he'd reported people beating him up and taking his food, that he was scared, upset, and having nightmares. "If you were in a place where people were taking advantage of you, don't you have to put up a fight?"

Landrum said, "That might be one way to respond."

"Imagine being locked up and brutalized . . . wouldn't you have to have backbone?"

"I would agree with that."

Black returned to the argument that the defendant suffered from organic brain damage. "People with brain damage can have poor judgment, explosive rage attacks?"

Landrum said, "Yes."

"In a neuropsychological interview, one should look for birth complications, learning disabilities, and the like?"

"Yes."

"In records at Savannas, they say, 'This is consistent with birth trauma and a near-drowning incident.' Did they say what was consistent?"

"Those are consistent with a finding of organic brain damage," the witness said.

Court recessed for the day. The following day, Wednesday, January 20, court resumed with Lynn Park's redirect of Dr. Landrum. Landrum felt that the nightmares Brancaccio reported having in jail were not hallucinations, that they might be a symptom of Post Traumatic Stress Disorder. Park said, "Did you diagnose him with that?"

"No."

"Were they before or after the murder?"

"After."

"Do they mean he didn't know what he was doing when he killed?"

"No."

"Do they mean he could not form the intent to kidnap and murder at the time?"

"No."

"Is he still competent to stand trial?"

"Yes."

"Does he know right from wrong?"

"Yes."

"Did Victor Brancaccio have the ability to form a specific intent to kidnap Mollie Frazier, take her behind the berm, and beat her to death?"

"Yes."

Dr. Daniel Martell was a forensic neuropsychiatrist, specializing in the relation of brain damage to criminal behavior. He'd published over twenty articles in prestigious peer-reviewed medical journals, all dealing with brain damage, mental disorder, and violent criminal behavior. Early on in his career, he'd interned at New York City's Bellevue Hospital, and in a maximum-security hospital for the criminally insane. More recently, he'd been affiliated with the Kirby Institute, among other hospitals and medical boards.

Zeroing in on that last, prosecutor Lynn Park asked, "People there are criminally insane?"

Martell said, "They've been found not guilty

by reason of insanity, or found not competent to stand trial."

"What if they become competent?"

"They go back to court."

"If someone insane became sane, would they be released?"

"Once they are in remission, they wouldn't be released to the street, but they would be sent to a less-secure environment."

"If someone were found to be sane, would they be kept in the hospital?"

"No."

The prosecution had asked the questions for the jury's benefit. Lynn Park had adroitly used the credentialed witness after establishing his expertise, as a vehicle to alert jurors to the possible consequences should they happen to find Victor Brancaccio not guilty by reason of insanity. He would go to a mental hospital. Should he later be found to have recovered his "sanity," he could and would ultimately be released back into the community.

In September 1995, Martell was called on to determine Brancaccio's mental state. "I reviewed all records, and examined him for two days. . . . I reviewed forty-seven different items, all police reports. I went to the site of the crime. I looked at the chronology of Victor's life, all school and medical records, the drowning incident, statements of witnesses, his statements. I looked at the psychiatric reports of other experts."

When he'd interviewed Brancaccio on Septem-

ber 14 and 15, 1995, the defendant was cooperative and eager to take the battery of psychological
tests. Martell said, "It felt manipulative. He came
in with an agenda, wanted things to be picked
up.

"In any forensic exam, you have to have some
suspicion. There could be incentives to get
money or stay out of trouble. You must test to
see if the subject is faking."

He'd given Brancaccio an I.Q. test, with the
defendant coming up in the low-average category.
Park asked if test results suggested Brancaccio
had organic brain damage. Martell said, "There's
no clear proof he has brain damage, it's possible
he might have brain damage, but I cannot point
to anything specific."

Park said, "In your experience, just because
there's a low I.Q. and learning disabilities, does
that mean brain damage?"

"No."

"What about Victor being mildly retarded?"

"Victor is absolutely not mildly retarded."

"Were you aware of any history of violence?"

"Yes. Victor had been violent many times,"
Martell said. Brancaccio had broken a school-
mate's nose. "He fought in the neighborhood,
he fought with his brother, he had a pattern of
fighting when his masculinity was questioned. He
had fifty-three different disciplinary referrals."

"Was the violent act of killing Mollie Frazier
out of character?"

"Out of character because he'd never killed before. It is consistent with his prior violence of smashing faces before."

Martell said that Brancaccio faked psychiatric test answers. "We did not get a valid response on the test because he faked it so badly. The test has scales built in to catch people trying to fake either that they're crazy, or trying to hide problems. He faked answers so badly that it rendered it uninterpretable.

"He tried to fake it to look crazy. It has checks to see if someone is faking. Brancaccio was selective in picking obvious items, but missed the subtle items. This was an indication he selectively picked crazy-sounding answers, but missed subtle items." Brancaccio was "pretending to be crazier than he is," Martell said. "For antisocial tendencies he was faking good, for self-deprecation he was faking bad. . . . In every test I gave to see if he's faking, he came out as faking."

Martell gave an example. "Let's say I show you a pen or a cup. Here's a pen. I hide them. Now, what did I show? A malingerer will say a cup. No, try again. I show him a cup, he says pen this time. Wrong again." It was the kind of test that even a blind person would get right fifty percent of the time.

"I gave Victor Brancaccio a similar test. He was wrong more than half the time. There's no way you can be wrong more than half the time. He was faking. . . . People that are faking will say all kinds of things. This tells me he was trying to look impaired."

Examining Brancaccio's different statements to friends and police about the crime, Martell said, "There were two versions. In the version he told to police, he downplayed what he did. When he told it to friends, he included more violent detail. To the police, he said he took Frazier by the arm and took her over the berm. To friends, he said he put her in a headlock. What he told police doesn't sound as bad."

Martell explained his methodology. "Forensic behavioral analysis is a fancy way of saying a way to see what goes on in a person's mind while committing a crime. Take a slow-motion look at what's happening in their mind, blow by blow of the crime. It's a good way to see if they know what they are doing and if they know it's wrong. It can be reconstructed by analyzing it moment by moment."

Martell's reconstructive analysis began with Brancaccio arguing with his mother. "He's angry. Brancaccio told me that when he gets angry, he likes to listen to rap. Rap is his angry music. He takes the toy gun and puts on rap music and goes for a walk to get away from his mom."

Brancaccio encountered Mollie Frazier, had an altercation with her. "He tells her, 'If you don't get out of my face, I'll hit you.' He tells police, 'I just got tired of it and hit her.' Let's look at that behavior. The fact that he gets angry is consistent with past behavior. His anger goes up and he makes a threat. He doesn't just whack her, he threatens her—then follows through.

"This tells me it was done on purpose. It's not impulsive, it's thought out. He made a decision to hit her on purpose."

Park said, "Anything tell you that he acted on impulse, on frenzy?"

"Not at this point."

"That he acted as a wild animal?"

"No."

"What else was significant?"

"After he strikes the first blow, he gets to another decision point in his behavior," Martell continued. "She tells him it hurts, threatens to call police. He says he knew it was wrong to hit her and he knew the right thing to do was say he was sorry. But he's also aware that he just got arrested.

"He knows he can do the right thing or the wrong thing. He told friends he decided to hurt her worse, to cause brain damage so she could not identify him. This tells me he knows what he is doing is wrong. . . .

"He makes an intentional decision to harm her further. He has to evaluate where he is. He's by the road, people can see her. In the open, he's at increased risk. He decides if he's going to hurt her worse, he's got to get out of sight. He drags her over the berm. He told police he dragged her by the arm. He told friends it was a headlock. It doesn't matter. What matters is she was dragged.

"Once he gets her behind the berm, he carries out his plan to cause brain damage. He kicks and beats her. She begs him, stop, stop, let's talk. His response is to say, f—— you. . . . He knows what he's doing and doesn't want to hear from her. He has an agenda. She says, please don't kill me. He says, shut up."

Martell analyzed the moment when Frazier offered Brancaccio a handkerchief to wipe her blood off his hand, to which he replied, "Bitch, do you have AIDS?" "While he was in Savannas, Brancaccio saw a video about AIDS. He is able to access, in the midst of the assault, the video he saw about AIDS. That shows me he is acutely aware of what he is doing, the nature and consequences of this."

After returning home, why didn't Brancaccio get rid of his bloody sneakers? "He was proud of those shoes; those were his Filas. He didn't want to throw away those shoes. Later, it was a bragging point," Martell said.

Brancaccio's mother asks, "Where have you been?" Brancaccio makes a decision to lie. He doesn't want to get caught. The next morning, he returns to the crime scene. "She was probably dead," Martell said, "but he reports to police she was still breathing. He may have thought or wished she was still alive.

"He collects his tape deck and throws the gun into the lake. He returns later to burn the body. His friends gave him advice. Now he's concerned about removing fingerprints. His thinking is, prints tie me to the crime. That shows he knows what he did was wrong."

Martell went on, "He's overwhelmed. Once

he's got a body, it's very perplexing about how to rid of it. He runs to his friends and brain-storms: run her over with a lawnmower, drive her into the lake. . . .

"He told friends he put 'Vaseline' on her. What's important was his intent to light her on fire and remove his fingerprints. When this does not work, he goes back to friends and discusses other plans. This shows lack of respect for the victim and lack of remorse." After weighing his options, Brancaccio decided that the most doable was to spray paint her.

Martell said, "Later he takes friends to see the body in a misguided effort on his part to garner respect. I'm a gangsta, I'm a bad guy. He says, I did some wild shit, I killed an old lady. He also talks about running away to New York City or It-aly. Finally, when caught by police, he lies about it, evidence that he knows it was wrong."

Park said, "Did the fact that he was taking Zoloft have an effect on his state of mind?"

"I have to preface by saying I'm not an M.D. and can't give an opinion about the chemistry of Zoloft," Martell said. "As far as this crime is con-cerned, I think it's irrelevant. He could have been on crack cocaine or heroin, it doesn't matter. Brancaccio knew what he was doing, knew it was wrong, and did it on purpose."

"In the legal sense, was he sane or insane at that time?"

"I think that's a question for the jury. He knew

what was wrong, but whether he was insane is for the jury to decide."

"He knew what he was doing? He could form a specific intent to commit the kidnapping and murder of Mollie Mae Frazier?"

"Yes."

Roy Black challenged Martell's conclusions, saying that they were based on false data: the statements of Victor Brancaccio. "You accept certain facts stated by Brancaccio to draw your opinion?"

Martell said, "Yes."

"If the facts are not right, that would diminish the accuracy of your opinion."

"That depends on the facts."

"If you rely on fact and the facts turn out to be different, then your opinion based on the facts diminishes in accuracy?"

"You've already asked that question and I've already answered it."

Black noted that Brancaccio said that after he'd hit her, Mollie Frazier said, "I didn't think you were this kind of person." "If this is untrue, would this not diminish the accuracy of your opinion?"

Martell said, "The critical issue is whether she said something about calling police."

Jack Zaccheo's statement was the source for Brancaccio's saying he planned to beat Frazier to give her brain damage, Black said. "If Jack said brain damage was never mentioned, would that change your opinion?"

PRESCRIPTION FOR MURDER

You are sure a Florida judge has made

"No."

"If after a number of blows, she said, 'Stop, let's talk about this,' she's still conscious—if it's not true, would that diminish the accuracy of your opinion?"

"Not necessarily," Martell said. "My opinion was the fact that he would disregard her pleas in a callous way, whether she was pleading or laying there wouldn't change the fact that he is trying to harm her. Even if she's unconscious, that doesn't change the fact that he hurt her."

"To you it was irrelevant whether he was under the influence of Zoloft, crack, or heroin, it wouldn't matter?"

"It wouldn't."

Black turned to some statements Brancaccio had made to Martell during their interviews. "He told you, 'I pray for the old lady every night. To this day I don't understand what made me do it'? Did he say that?"

Martell said, "Yes."

" 'I'm not this kind of person'—did he say that?"

"Yes. He had an agenda of what he wanted me to hear that was part of it."

"Did he say, 'I feel remorse'?"

"Yes."

Black tried to neutralize Martell's earlier testimony by alluding to the possibility that if Brancaccio was found insane and put in a mental hospital, he might later be found sane and returned to the street. "You are aware a Florida judge has to rule someone is no longer a danger to be released?"

Martell said, "Sure."

"That decision is not just made by doctors?"

"No."

Black said, "You also said Victor did not exhibit remorse."

"Yes."

"Do you remember him saying that the next day when he saw the body, he had tears in his eyes?"

"Yes."

"Remember him saying, 'I felt bad for her'?"

"What he says to police is a more benevolent, caring story than what he tells friends, which is a little more malevolent and unkind," Martell said.

Park's redirect established the existence of a test which examined children who'd almost drowned, with five factors used to predict who'd have brain damage. Martell said, "If you had two or less, there was a less than ninety percent chance of having brain damage. Victor had one of those factors.

"My thinking about brain damage and violent behavior is that too often people want to use brain damage as an excuse. It is never all by itself the cause, except during a seizure, people might flail out and hit someone, but it is not intentional.

"This beating had logic to it."

The state rested its rebuttal case.

* * *

Closings began on the eighth day, Thursday, January 21, at 9:30 A.M., with prosecution and defense ready to put the best spin on the mountain of facts the trial had laid out before the jury. Had Victor Brancaccio known what he was doing every step of the way, making a number of decisions leading to the kidnapping and murder of Mollie Frazier? Or was he a borderline case, near retarded, suffering from organic brain damage, whose Zoloft prescription had deranged his thinking, catapulting him into a wild frenzy during which the kidnapping and murder occurred?

Lynn Park's closing began powerfully, as the prosecutor indicated the state's exhibits belonging to the deceased. "This is all that's left of Mollie Frazier . . . shorts and shirt, some peppermint candy, the eyeglasses, a hearing aid. Frazier's life ended on June eleventh, while taking a walk in the early evening. She met up with the defendant and he ended her life that summer night."

Brancaccio had an altercation with Frazier, then, "He tells her, 'Don't say anything, I'm going to hit you.' He hits her, by his own words, hits her in the head. There they are, out on the roadside, within sight of his own house. Does he beat her in an uncontrollable frenzy there? No, he stops and thinks, she's gonna tell his parents, cops."

He took her behind the berm and beat her to death, fleeing when he thought he heard a car.

"He gets scared. He knew he'd done something wrong. He leaves her there to die in the field and then Victor goes on with his life." At around eight-thirty that night, he calls Kristin Bonpartito, telling her he just hit an old lady. Since last talking to her earlier that day, "he's gone out, met with Frazier, beaten her, and now he's ready to go party with the girls."

While wrestling around with Kristin Bonpartito, he'd smelled her skin lotion, saying, "You smell like the old lady." Look at his demeanor, Park said. "He wasn't crying, he wasn't upset. He was just trying to act like a big guy. He said, 'You guys didn't believe what I said? Good, I just wanted to see what you'd say.' He'd bring the subject up during the night, and then it was 'just kidding'—the little brother type, hanging out."

After painting the body, he'd told Jack Zaccheo and Lynette Winchester, "She's all red now." Park scoffed at the suggestion that Zaccheo was the reason Brancaccio tried to burn the body. When Zaccheo said to the defendant, "You are going to leave the body in the front yard!" he was in disbelief.

"Murder does not always make sense. There is no motive here," Park said.

She reminded jurors that when Sergeant D'Agostino had arrested him, Brancaccio said, "You got the wrong guy," more proof that he knew what he did was wrong. Was Brancaccio's confession given voluntarily? On the tape, jurors heard the defendant say he'd read and understood the waiver form he'd signed. "Then he says it's all new to him and that he did not do it," Park said. "When he thinks there is evidence that is going to tie him to murder, he says he has to tell the truth."

Park refuted the defense's claim that Brancaccio suffered from organic brain damage. "They said he was premature and underweight, but he was not that premature and not that underweight. . . . Appel and Schlensky are the only ones that say he is mildly retarded. With Martell, he scores not retarded. There are lots of kids with learning disabilities who know right from wrong. Victor knew right from wrong and the consequences. . . .

"They say he became a beast who could not control himself, yet when he went home, he was sane when he talked to his mother." Park added that Appel and Schlensky did not agree with each other on certain points.

Jurors had heard lots of testimony about malingering, that is, faking symptoms. Park said, "Martell did a test to determine if Victor was malingering. There was a pattern of malingering on the psychiatric test. Landrum also detected malingering, saying that Brancaccio chose not to perform at optimal level.

"The defendant is a liar, a malingerer, and a murderer. He knew exactly what he was doing, he knew right from wrong, and he intended to beat Mollie Frazier to the point where she could not remember."

The defense's Roy Black opened his closing not by minimizing, but rather highlighting the horrific nature of the crime to point out his client's mental state. "There is no overlooking how terrible this is. This was not the act of a reasonable, logical, sane person. It was senseless and without reason. . . . People do not do something like this unless there was something behind it. This is the act of a diseased, damaged brain. We look to make sense of it, but there is none because it is the product of a damaged mind.

"There is no purpose to it; it is utterly bizarre."

Black argued that just because the defendant could carry out some events with seeming sanity didn't mean he was sane. The fact that someone in a mental house may be able to get out of bed and go to the bathroom didn't mean that person was sane. Brancaccio had killed Mollie Frazier in a frenzy.

He said, "What evidence can we rely on? Hobin says when looking at the injuries, that he thinks it was a quick violent outburst, a seemingly unprovoked attack without motive. The blows were done in seconds. She could have died after the first blow. On redirect, Mr. Mirman asked, 'About how long did the incident take?' Hobin said it happened in a matter of seconds."

Black said that he believed that Frazier was unconscious and did not speak after she was hit in the head. Martell had used statements she could not have made to bolster his claim that Brancaccio knew right from wrong. Jack Zaccheo's statement that Brancaccio had told him that he planned to beat Frazier to give her brain damage was also not credible. "Zaccheo is not on trial, but he has no believability. I think he did more than he admits."

That last drew an objection from the prosecution, which was overruled, the judge finding that Black could say what he believed. Black said, "I believe it based on what I have seen. If you take what Zaccheo has done, I do not think he is believable."

Zaccheo had said that Brancaccio said that he'd dragged Frazier over the berm. Black disputed that, saying there was no evidence at the roadside of dragging, and that Hobin had looked for bruises on Frazier's arms and other evidence of dragging and found none.

The prosecution had put on witnesses like Martell, who described Brancaccio's mental processes regarding things which plainly couldn't have happened, Black said. Frazier could not have asked Brancaccio not to kill her—she would have been unable to talk from the blows to the head. As for her offering him a handkerchief to wipe the blood and him responding, "Bitch, do you have AIDS?" Black said the chances of it happening were "virtually zero. Evidence? No, this is delusional. . . . They take it and accept it as a fact."

Voice rising, Black scorned the prosecution's theory that Brancaccio's remark about AIDS was inspired by a sexual-hygiene video he'd seen in Savannas. "Victor watched a video about safe sex, so that proves it must have happened—?! I cannot believe that this evidence could be used in America in 1999!"

As for charges that Brancaccio had tried to cover up his crime, the reverse was true; there'd never been a crime that had less of a cover-up, with the defendant running around telling all his friends what he'd done. The botched burning and spray painting of the body to cover up fingerprints hadn't been Brancaccio's "weighing his options," as prosecutors claimed. It came from Jack Zaccheo, Black claimed, when Zaccheo said, "Look, you can't leave a body there."

Brancaccio tells Kristin Bonpartito that he thinks he hit an old lady; he tells Angel Pellot, not a friend but a mere acquaintance, what he did and shows him the blood on his sneakers. Black said, " 'Let me show you the evidence.' This is the man who's doing a cover-up? I don't think so. He's leadable, he follows the suggestions of other people, does it in the way that somebody with a diseased brain would. He doesn't do it in any logical way. It's totally without sense."

Prescribing drugs for people with brain damage can be difficult and requires careful monitoring. Victor Brancaccio's brain was different from those of normal people. The side effects of Zoloft on a brain like his can be, and were, dangerously unpredictable. Dr. Martell himself had said in one of his research papers that people with brain damage sometimes had incidents of unprovoked rage attacks, explosive in nature. When asked what would happen if someone on Zoloft did a crime, Matthews had said it would be a quick attack. "Schlensky says Zoloft is the straw that broke the camel's back," Black said.

Prosecutors said that past violence was a precursor of future violence and that Brancaccio's history of violence before Zoloft foreshadowed his violence after taking the drug. Black scoffed at the data they'd used to establish Brancaccio's history of violence. The October 1992 fight, where he'd broken the other youth's nose, was "a typical teenage fight," Black said. "Teens fight all the time. It is not a precursor to homicide.

"They said he had fights with his brother; that's hardly evidence of homicide. He stole beer and was involuntarily admitted to the hospital. I am not saying he is perfect. He has brain damage. Should we expect anything less?"

Could it be proven that Zoloft was the catalyst for Brancaccio's crime? Black said, "Victor had all of the symptoms—paranoia, delusions, aggression. Zoloft is given him on top of his brain-damaged mind. If the crime was Zoloft driven, it would be out of control."

The "urge to kill" which Brancaccio said he'd experienced in prison was explained by the hellish torment he suffered there—beaten by other prisoners, feces thrown at him, attempted sodomy. That was why Brancaccio had not done his best on one of the tests given him by Landrum, because he was distracted by his victimization in jail.

Black scorned the circumstances leading to Brancaccio's confession after his arrest on Monday, June 14. With his suggestible nature, Brancaccio had been influenced to tailor his story to the evidence which Detective Scott Beck had told him the police had. "This couldn't have happened if he'd had a lawyer there. I don't think you can rely upon any of it. . . . Victor gives at least nine versions of what happened. . . . Even Zaccheo says he can't believe Victor says one thing and contradicts it in the next sentence."

Of the prosecution, Black said, "They're going to say that Victor made choices. Choices! He didn't chose to be born like that. You think he chose to flunk the first grade? Imagine what it was like for this kid to go to school, go to learning-disabled classes. He didn't choose those kind of things.

"There's no excuse for what Victor did, but when you look at this, you have to wonder how this could happen. . . . I don't know what went on out on that street. There's no way to know. I do know I've never seen an act so senseless, so motiveless, without any reason or rationale.

"How could this happen? People who have brain damage have unprovoked rage. Some people who take Zoloft have frenzied reactions."

This crime was the product of no normal mind,

Black argued. "How can we say that he's responsible, that he acted evilly, that he had intent to commit these crimes? I don't think he did. It does not minimize them to find Victor guilty by reason of insanity. It doesn't let him off the hook.

"There's something more involved here than just a case of murder. You just have to say that this is a product of his life. His brain damage, some effect of the medication, caused this brutality that's unexplainable."

Black expressed the hope that jurors would see the crime as "the motiveless act of a brain-damaged young man," concluding, "the only rational explanation is a moment of insanity. This boy should not be sent back to prison. He ought to be sent to a mental hospital, where he can get treatment. Maybe sometime can be done for him. I just hope you consider it. Thank you."

The prosecution had the right of rebuttal, the final say. Lynn Park professed indignation at Black's disdain for the police tactics used to get Brancaccio's confession. She reminded jurors that Florida law did not require that the parent be notified and the judge had ruled that they'd be able to consider Brancaccio's statement in their deliberations.

Asking the jury to consider the facts and decide on the evidence, Park said, "You're the fact finders. Don't decide on sympathy. You've had a picture painted of a sad, pathetic defendant. Mr. Black said the defendant went around telling everybody. He didn't tell everybody—he told people he thought were his friends. He's attention seeking.

"You're going to have to look at the big picture. Nobody said Brancaccio is bright and smart, or a gifted student. His I.Q. is in the borderline range, but he's not retarded. Look at what he does. He lives a pretty normal life, he's not so brain damaged he doesn't know right from wrong. He does."

Brancaccio was a malingerer. Park said, "The defendant faked. He's a faker, he's a liar. He said he didn't know he was on the North American continent. Well, he told Zaccheo, 'They're not gonna catch me, I'll go to New York or Italy.' He knew where New York was, he knew where Italy was."

Park addressed the question of the defendant's sanity. "Dr. Schlensky said the drug pushed him over the edge, Zoloft pushed him over the edge and he went into a frenzy, becoming this wild beast. Then when he went back home, he was sane, and that he's sane now."

But while in jail, Brancaccio said he felt the "urge to kill." Park said, "He says he wants to kill again: 'I want to feel the high of killing again.' He's not on Zoloft. He wants to kill again and he's not on Zoloft.

"Mr. Black says this was a moment of insanity, and keeps referring to brain damage and depression. Don't assume because it's said over and over that he is so brain damaged. He might be to some degree. People who regain their sanity don't stay in hospitals. They go back out on the streets."

Victor Brancaccio had a history, including nine suspensions from public school, the October 1992 fight, petty theft. When he was admitted to Savannas Hospital, Lina Brancaccio had told staffers that Brancaccio was having temper outbursts, running away, burning himself, and failing school. His psychiatric history describes him as aggressive since 1992, fights with his brother, depressed, angry and anxious. He'd said, "I get angry and want to kill my brother."

The defense had spent an hour and a half attacking Dr. Martell's testimony, Park said. "Why? Because Martell was able to sit here and explain the defendant's behavior and state of mind so clearly that anybody could understand it. He showed how Brancaccio knew what he was doing. He knew it was wrong, knew he'd get in trouble. He formed the intent to kidnap Frazier and take her from the roadside to where he'd be able to beat her."

She tackled the issue of motive. "Mr. Black says there is no motive, he says it is irrational. This might be one of them: sometimes evil things are done by evil people. Maybe his motive was to experience the high of killing. He was mad at his mother and took it out on Mollie Frazier."

How could jurors determine what was credible in Brancaccio's confession? Park said, "Mr. Black said you cannot rely on Victor's statement, but you can rely on the crime scene. You need to take the statement Victor made and see what did he say that can be corroborated by some other evidence. Mrs. Simcsuk said she saw both of them by the road, so you can rely on it when he says he was walking and met Mollie Frazier. He says he had a black plastic gun. This was found at the scene, part of it was lying under Frazier. You can rely on that.

"He said he hit her with the gun, he told Detective Beck he hit her. You can rely on that. The gun was in pieces and on one of them Nippes found a white head hair that had been forcibly removed. So you can rely on that statement, yes."

Brancaccio had said he'd hit her on the right side of the head, and photos showed lacerations there. He said that she had two hearing aids. When she was found, one was still in her ear and the other had fallen out. He said she took out a tissue to wipe the blood. A bloody tissue was found at the scene. He said he spray painted her, the spray paint found at his house matched that on the body.

Park went on, "Beck asked if Brancaccio knew what he did was wrong and he said he did. . . . The kidnapping was important. Victor took her from the side of the road to a secluded area where he could beat her until she would not remember. If he's uncontrollable and in a frenzy and could not control himself, he would beat her to death right there.

"He did not do it, because he is thinking. He was already in trouble for the beer incident. He does not want her to go to the police. He knows he is going to get in trouble. If he did not have the presence of mind to stop, he would have done the whole thing right there. He beat her at the road and he takes her out of sight where no one will see her. He knew he should have helped her.

"He made the decision, he had evil intent. He beat her to death. He hit her over the head with the gun, smashing the gun. . . . This is the result of the evil intention—he did it so she would not remember. It is time he be held responsible. He abducted her, he forced her behind the berm for the purpose of inflicting harm.

"He committed felony murder."

So ended the closings. Court was recessed for the day, the judge ruling that deliberations would begin on Friday morning. The following day, jurors were charged with their instructions, proceeding to the jury room to begin their deliberations. Five hours later, they emerged with a verdict.

The bailiff handed the jury's verdict to the judge, who read it through. The judge handed it to the clerk. "The clerk will publish the verdict."

"We the jury find the defendant, Victor Brancaccio, as to count one, guilty of first-degree murder as charged in the indictment. As to count two, guilty of kidnapping as charged in the indictment."

After the verdict was announced, Lina Brancaccio fainted. Family members put water on her face.

The judge thanked the jury, court was adjourned and the trial was over.

After the verdict, a press conference was held. A rueful Roy Black reacted to the verdict. "Insanity is probably the least possible verdict to consider. I thought it would have been the legitimate and correct verdict." He opined that there were grounds for appeal because the police "lied" to Brancaccio about contacting his parents, and said that he would "probably" be handling the appeal.

A reporter asked how his client took the verdict. Black said, "Victor is twenty-two or twenty-three but has the mental age of fourteen or fifteen. I don't know if it's hit home. We'll talk to him. It's not easy talking to him."

Black told *Court TV,* "I realize that it's probably a futile hope that our society would treat people like Victor well. It's just not going to happen. We're not going to spend the money, the time, the effort, the medications, the testing, everything that needs to be done.

"But I think rather than throw him in a cell, where he's going to be in the state penitentiary here with people who are going to victimize him and have tried to victimize him for several years, I would personally feel a lot better, at least, if he was in a mental institution. I would think society is doing something for him rather than treating him like a dog and torturing him in the state penitentiary."

Prosecutor Lynn Park said, "Roy Black is a good lawyer, but the facts were on our side, the evidence was on our side." Told that the defense planned to appeal, she said she was not surprised, but she was sure that the conviction would stand. "Roy Black is very persuasive and made persuasive arguments, so we had to come out strong and show Brancaccio is not brain damaged. The jury saw he's got some evil in him. It's not brain damage and depression and a drug that made him do this."

Asked what the state would do if Brancaccio's confession were suppressed, she said it would make the trial more difficult, but noted that a suppression hearing in 1993 had already addressed most of the issues, ruling for the prosecution.

A reporter said, "You agree he has mental problems?"

Park said, "He had major depression. They diagnosed him with mental problems."

"Is prison a place for a person with mental infirmities?"

"He may have mental problems, but not such that he can't function like normal people. Depression is common in prison. Victor Brancaccio needs to be in a structured environment. Prison is the place for him, not a mental hospital, where they have the option of releasing him."

Park told *Court TV* her theory of the crime. "Anger. I think Victor has a temper he cannot control. He struck out at Mrs. Frazier following the argument with his mother. There was a lot of violence that went on within that home. The mother made a comment that she felt like a punching bag. And she's caught in the middle of these male figures within her home. There was a lot of fighting that went on between the dad and his older brother Albert.

"Victor left the home after fighting with his mother and the first person he encountered was Mollie Frazier, another female authority figure. And that's what triggered him. You know if she said something to him, looked at him wrong, whatever it was, that triggered him to strike out at her." Although they lived in close proximity, there was no indication that Brancaccio and Frazier knew each other, Park said.

"The family is well known to law enforcement. The Brancaccio family has had police officers respond to their home due to violence in the past. . . . It seems to be a family that is rather volatile and things are handled within that family in a way that lends itself to violence. And I think that's what Victor has seen growing up, and so he has chosen to handle his problems with violence. He's an evil person who attacked this elderly woman for absolutely no reason and then beat her to the point that she died."

"You think he's evil?"

"I think Victor Brancaccio is an evil man and he should never, ever be out on the street."

"What about insanity?"

"First of all, Brancaccio was not insane." Park said that except for Appel, all the other experts did not find him to be insane. If he were insane at the time of the killing, he wouldn't have known he did something wrong, wouldn't know the consequences of what he was doing. "And clearly he did. But if they were to say, yes, he was insane at the time he did this, but he's not insane now, how would you hold someone in any facility, a mental-health facility, if they were not insane?

"So he would be released, he would be on the street. And it was important to try to get the jury to understand that. And I think we did do that."

What was the key evidence?

"I would say that the key evidence in this case was Jan Simcsuk actually seeing them on the side of the road. That way we placed them in one location," Park said. "That and the fact that the gun was found under her body, at least part of it. There were small pieces kind of strewn around and a large part of the gun underneath her body with a little bit just sticking out. And then when it was spray painted, that had the paint on it."

Details were made public about what had gone on in the jury room during deliberations. Early on, ten of the twelve jurors were ready to convict, but there were two holdouts, a man and woman, who thought that some of the bizarre circumstances of the crime and the defendant's conduct after the crime indicated that Brancaccio might indeed be insane. What clinched the argument in favor of conviction was the fact that Brancaccio had taken Frazier over the berm to beat her to death, showing that he was not in a frenzy, but rather knew that what he was doing was wrong and that's why he was taking her where they would not be seen. The guilty verdict was unanimous.

In a final stinging twist, jurors learned what had been carefully kept from them throughout the trial, namely that theirs was not the first but the second trial of Victor Brancaccio for murder and kidnapping. Held in 1995, presided over by Judge Dwight Geiger, with the same prosecution team and Juan Torres, but not Roy Black, for the defense, the first trial had ended in a guilty verdict, but that verdict was later set aside due to a technicality. A second trial in October 1998 had gotten off to a false start when a prospective juror had said in open court in front of other prospective jurors that Brancaccio had been found guilty of murder and kidnapping in 1995. The trial was called off, resulting in the trial held in January 1999.

After the second trial, the Brancaccios reactivated their civil suit against Savannas Hospital for releasing Victor Brancaccio too soon and improperly monitoring him while he was on Zoloft.

A month after the verdict in the second trial, Victor Brancaccio was sentenced to life in prison for murder and kidnapping. On the murder charge, he'll be eligible for parole in twenty-five years. The kidnapping charge does not permit parole, so Brancaccio will never be released.

Let the last word on the case be that of the female juror who said, "I didn't want to take a chance that this guy would ever be out in the street again to meet another woman walking in her neighborhood and to have the same thing happen again."

Arkansas v. *Stocks:*

THE SCOUTMASTER'S SECRET

THE CRIME OF MURDER

An iceberg hides seven-eighths of itself below the surface. Sometimes, too, so does a homicide. The brutal triple-slaying which rocked Lonoke, Arkansas, was merely the prelude to an onslaught of shocking revelations about an evil that had preyed for two generations on perhaps one hundred victims, a sinister force which could and did reach into almost any household and tear it apart.

Located in eastern Arkansas, in the Little Rock area, Lonoke (pronounced "lone oak"), population 4500, is a farming community whose main products are rice, soy beans, and fish. (A nearby site on Highway 70 boasts the world's largest fish farm.) With its handsomely restored courthouse, many churches, well-kept homes, and surrounding farmlands, Lonoke embodies the appeal and values of small-town America. A Southern town in its rhythms and way of life, it's a place where everybody knows everybody else. By and large, its open, friendly folk are socially conservative in many ways, believers in the virtues of such time-honored institutions as church, home, school, flag, and the Boy Scouts.

Joe Stocks and his wife, Barbara, were lifelong Lonoke residents. Their two children were Heath, twenty, and Heather, eighteen. Heath Stocks was handsome, athletic, a former Eagle Scout, and star player on a Lonoke high school football team that had won the state championship. Heather Stocks was pretty, popular, a straight-A student, and high school cheerleader, who'd been elected class valedictorian and invited to attend Harvard. Since going away to attend Henderson University in Arkadelphia, Heath Stocks had hit some rough patches. Now, he'd flunked out of school. Worse, he was in trouble with the law. Nothing big, but even small scrapes with the authorities were expensive.

He dreaded telling the bad news to his father. He dreaded his father. Whatever else his virtues, Joe Stocks was hot-tempered and abusive to his son. He was a long-haul trucker whose job required him to be away from the family for lengthy stretches of time, and when he returned, it always seemed to Heath that he brought hard, painful punishment with him.

Joe Stocks believed in corporal punishment where Heath was concerned and, according to

Heath, whipped him with belts, chains, switches and the like, beating the boy's bare buttocks until the blood flowed.

That Joe Stocks had a temper was something with which even his mother would agree. In an interview, Dorothy Stocks, Joe's mother and Heath's grandmother, said, "Joe had a very bad temper. . . . I was over there several times, I would get to the door . . . and I would hear Joe's voice booming. Angry. I might go in. I might turn around and go back. Come back home. I never said anything to him about his temper. His dad's temper was bad. So I lived with it. . . .

"What goes on behind closed doors, in a family's home, you don't know what goes on behind those closed doors. Everything can be fine when you're out in public. Nothing shows up whatsoever. So I just don't know. I don't know.

"But I do know Joe had a horrible temper."

She said that Heath came under a lot of parental pressure. "He was pushed to do his best. And he made good grades in school. He was well liked. But there was always this: you've got to do better. You've got to go to college, and be out where you can get a job at $50,000 a year. Well, you don't start out at $50,000 a year. And he had had this stuff poked at him and prodded at him."

Heath was now old enough for college, but there was still real tension between him and his father. He felt that in his father's eyes, he could do no right.

Coming home on Friday afternoon at about

four-thirty, he was relieved to find Joe Stocks out of the house, still at work. His mother was making dinner, cooking steak and mushrooms in a crock pot. Later, she and her husband would be taking cheerleader daughter Heather to a high school basketball game. Barbara Stocks told Heath that his grandparents had invited him to join them and some other relatives for dinner. Adding to the occasion was the presence of Joe Stocks's brother, James T. Stocks, visiting from California.

Heath Stocks went to his grandparents' house, which was nearby. Present were Martin and Dorothy Stocks, Uncle James Stocks, and Aunt Bonnie Moody. The foursome plus Heath went to dinner at the Western Sizzlin' restaurant. During the meal, Heath sufficiently unbent to tell the others something of his troubles. At college in Arkadelphia, he'd been drinking a lot, too much. He'd flunked out. He'd been arrested for DWI. In a separate incident, he'd confronted someone whom he blamed for stealing his motorcycle helmet. The police had stepped in, arresting him for making "terroristic threats" to the other.

The legal troubles could be handled; all it took was money, specifically $3500, the amount his legal fines were going to cost. That's was all. But it only added to the family's troubles. An accident a few months earlier had laid up Joe Stocks, leaving him unable to work. He'd only recently gone back, making money again, and there were a lot of bills that needed catching up on. Heath was also concerned that the arrests would prevent him from joining the military. He wanted to become a Navy SEAL.

Still, it seemed to Dorothy Stocks that her grandson had enjoyed himself during the dinner.

Martin and Dorothy Stocks went home. Heath went in, used the bathroom, and came back out, saying, "Well, Grandma, I'm going home." It was about eight P.M. when he left.

At 10:15 P.M., Joe and Barbara Stocks dropped in at his parents' house. Martin Stocks broached the subject of Heath's fines. Joe Stocks, furious, said that if Heath couldn't pay the fine by himself, "he could stay in jail."

Wife in tow, Joe Stocks headed home for what promised to be a memorable father-son confrontation.

At about ten-thirty P.M., a 911 call was received by the Lonoke County Sheriff's Office. The female dispatcher answered the 911 phone, but the caller wasn't there. The 911 phone had caller ID, putting the caller's name and address up on a screen. The call had come from the Stockses' family residence. The dispatcher called the number back, but the line was busy. Two minutes later, there was a second 911 call from the same source, which when answered, again had no one on the other end of the line. The dispatcher immediately sent a deputy to the residence. One was already in the area, so he arrived quickly.

Arriving at the Stockses' house, and receiving

no answer to his knock, the deputy went through the carport door, into the house. The door opened on a kitchen. There he saw bodies and blood.

Murder happens in small towns, too, but this was slaughter, a massacre. The cordite stench of gunsmoke hung in the air. On the kitchen floor lay three dead bodies. The deputy backed out and called the dispatcher, who called Sheriff Charles "Charlie" Martin, who was on the scene within ten minutes of receiving the call.

Lonoke County Sheriff Charlie Martin, big, bluff, open faced, had only recently been elected to the office. Martin knew the Stockses. Heath Stocks was a friend of the sheriff's two sons. They'd slept over at each other's houses. One of his deputies was best friends with Joe Stocks.

Sheriff Martin described the scene to *Court TV.* "Blood was everywhere. There was a big pool of blood around Joe and Barbara Stocks. Joe was laying at the east end of the bar. Barbara was laying—as you look, you're looking down into a hallway. Barbara was laying head towards Joe, kind of in the hallway. Heather was laying back against the bar, between both of them."

The house was in chaos: a golf club had been rammed through the TV screen, drawers removed from cabinets and their contents dumped on the floor, closets and bureaus ransacked.

The phone line was stretched around a set of French doors, into another part of the room where Heather lay. The phone cord was wound around her and the phone lay nestled against her throat. Part of her finger had been shot. Heather was the one who'd made the 911 calls.

From the way the place was torn up, the rage it displayed, Sheriff Martin guessed that the killer was either a family member or a jilted boyfriend. He hadn't heard of Heather Stocks having any trouble with jilted boyfriends.

The interviewer asked, "Where was Heath?"

"Where was Heath? Heath wasn't there," Martin said. "Heath was in Arkadelphia, or on his way to Arkadelphia. I suspect he was on his way back to Arkadelphia whenever we found the crime scene. The deputy couldn't have missed him by more than three or four minutes."

Heath Stocks had to be found. Within the first twenty-four hours, as information came in on Stocks's movements on Friday, he became the prime suspect. Martin recalled, "With my family, especially my sons, they couldn't believe that Heath had done something like this. Thought that we can't be right. There were things I couldn't tell them. It was just hard for a time. My sons, you know, just kind of stayed back away from me. Until they had to finally face the fact that yes, he did do this."

Arkadelphia police searched for Stocks. Three officers went to the apartment of one of his friends. Stocks lay there on a couch. He asked if the lawmen had come about some of his outstanding traffic tickets. That struck a false note, since Stocks should have known that three offi-

cers wouldn't have come on that kind of complaint. They'd come for him, and they took him
away, bringing him back to Lonoke, where he was
interviewed by a Lonoke County Sheriff's Office
detective and an Arkansas State Police investigator. He confessed that night.

Stocks had gotten rid of the gun in Arkadelphia, throwing it in the Caddo River. Behind a
Pizza Hut and in a nearby creek, Arkadelphia investigators found jewelry which he'd taken from
the house, and a pair of gloves he'd worn when
the shooting took place.

He'd killed them all, Stocks said, his father,
mother, and sister. He told police a strange tale.

He'd flunked out of school and had moved out
of the dorm. For the past week, he'd been living
at a friend's place in Arkadelphia and had returned home to Lonoke for the weekend. He was
still in the process of moving his stuff back home,
and on Friday, January 17, he'd brought back a
carload of his belongings. When he got home at
about four-thirty P.M., his dad was out working,
driving a truck. His mother was home, cooking
dinner. Sister Heather was getting ready for the
basketball game. He left the house at about five-
thirty, going over to his grandparents' house and
from there going out to dinner with his relatives.

Coming home after the meal, he said, his good
spirits began to dull. He sat around watching TV,
getting more and more angry. He told police, "I

was just watching TV. . . . I started thinking about all the trouble my dad and I were having, and I started crying and I started getting mad. The longer I sat there, the angrier I got. I can't explain that."

He put a golf club through the TV screen. Then, he said, "I got a .45-caliber automatic pistol that my dad kept in his gun cabinet and another clip. I put that extra clip in my pocket."

The .45 was a lot of gun, but he knew how to handle it. In recent years he'd become quite proficient in the use of firearms.

He said that after that, he didn't remember much of what happened, just bits and pieces.

He stalked through the house, tearing drawers from cabinets and dumping their contents on the floor. He said, "I carried the gun with me as I went from room to room, messing up the house. All the time I was doing this, I kept thinking and kept getting mad. After I messed up the house, I tried to kill myself."

He knelt on the living room floor with the gun in his mouth, he said, trying to work up the nerve to pull the trigger. He took the gun out of his mouth, put it back in, and once more took it out.

That's how his sister found him. Heather Stocks came in the house first, alone, at ten-thirty P.M. Taking in the way the place had been turned upside down, she may have thought that it had been hit by burglars. She picked up the phone and started to call 911. This was the first call to register at the station.

Stocks told her not to call. She hung up the phone. He told her to get out of the house. She didn't complete the call, but she didn't leave the house, either.

Stocks said, "I remember being on the living room floor, with the gun in my mouth. My sister came home. And when she walked through the door and she walked in the kitchen, she turned and looked at me. And she asked me what was wrong. I told her to leave. Told her to get out and leave. And she asked me again, she said, 'What's—what's wrong?' I remember going back in the living room, getting down on my knees, and sticking the gun in my mouth."

About two minutes later, Stocks said, his parents entered. "At this time, Mom and Dad came in the carport door. They both saw how the house was messed up, and I think Mom said, call 911. I saw Dad with the phone in his hand and I started shooting. I shot my dad first, and I just kept on shooting until Mom, Dad and Heather were all on the floor. I remember shooting my dad in the head after he was on the floor, but I don't remember shooting the others after they were down.

"Next thing I know, they're all dead. They're all laying there. . . ."

He didn't remember shooting Heather, but she was down, too. He wished he hadn't done it, and prayed for them all to come back to life, he said.

He ran. He got out of the house, barely a few minutes ahead of the first deputy to arrive. He fled to Arkadelphia, where he threw the gun in the Caddo River, and dropped some other things in a Dumpster.

When he was arrested, the first person he asked to speak to was his Boy Scout troop leader, Jack Walls.

In small towns, family is important, and few families in Lonoke were more important than the Wallses. Charles Walls, Jr., eighty, owned a good part of the businesses in town. An attorney who'd risen to city judge, then justice of the peace, in 1995 he was appointed to the newly created position of Lonoke County Circuit Judge, which paid a handsome annual sum of $100,000. Harder to set a price on, but more valuable by far, was his chain of friendships and associations with other town, city, and state powerbrokers, the insiders' clique.

The octogenarian jurist was known to his intimates as "Junior," while his son, Charles Walls III, fifty-two, was known as "Jack." No less than his father, Jack Walls was actively engaged in Lonoke's vitals. In 1969, Walls had dropped out of law school in Fayetteville to go to fight in Vietnam, returning a few years later. He'd gone to work at the Remington Arms Company factory, where he now held the post of supervisor. He was athletic, with close-cropped, thinning, fair hair. Sometimes he wore aviator-type glasses. He was married, with three daughters.

Walls was an enthusiastic and vigorous adult volunteer for the Boy Scouts of America, holding the rank of Assistant Scoutmaster of Troop #103. He was also an adult leader of the Scouts' elite Order of the Arrow or Brotherhood. Popular with kids and parents alike, he'd been involved with scouting for close to a quarter century, shaping the lives of the many boys who'd come under his charge.

Scouting was important in Lonoke, an integral part of a boy's life-style. Adults were pretty much agreed in thinking that it helped build character, problem-solving abilities, and teamwork, instilling youth with the values of respect, honor, and obedience. At the third-grade level, boys were eligible to join the Cub Scouts. Moving up through the ranks, they'd graduate to the Boy Scouts, with its local camp-outs and national camporees, like the ones held periodically on Boy Scouts land in Philmott, New Mexico.

Scout leader Jack Walls cared about kids, about people. He was always ready to help out a neighbor, friend, or youngster. He was a popular leader. Everybody wanted to be in his troop, the boys all but worshipped him. When one of them had a problem, Walls would be there for him, often spending hours just helping the lad talk it out.

Honoring his work and countless contributions to youth, the Lonoke Chamber of Commerce had voted him Man of the Year. Mark Buffalo, a reporter for the Lonoke *Democrat,* recalled, "I hate to say he was like a god to these children, but at the same time, he could have been. He had that kind of control of them. And in particular, with Heath Stocks."

Walls and his wife, Pam, were good friends with Joe and Barbara Stocks. An Eagle Scout, Heath Stocks had been in scouting's elite Order of the Arrow. Heath Stocks was close to Jack Walls, closer to him it seemed than to his own father.

In the aftermath of the murders, Walls volunteered to stay overnight in the Stockses' home to secure it against curiosity seekers, vandals, and thieves, an offer the police gladly accepted. Technically, the house was a crime scene, but what the hell, they had the killer, even if it was hard to believe it was Heath Stocks.

A few days after the killings, but before he'd gotten in to see Heath Stocks in jail, Walls attended a meeting that was held at a house at Greers Ferry Lake, to brief friends and relatives of the Stockses about developments in the case. At that meeting, one of the first things Walls said was, "Did Heath implicate anybody in the murders when he was arrested?" as though he thought Stocks might have had an accomplice.

The trial wasn't much. Acting on the advice of his public defender, Heath Stocks pled guilty and received three life sentences, with no parole. He began serving his time.

A young man snaps, kills his possibly abusive father and his mother and sister, and spends the rest of his life behind bars, while outside, stunned townfolk try to put it behind them and get on with the healing, moving forward. That's how it should have ended, but it didn't.

Jack Vincent, then a reporter for TV station KARK, later observed, "This story has so many twists and turns and spins to it, it's crazy, it's beyond belief. They say truth is stranger than fiction, and in this case that was simply exactly the way it was."

THE EARLIER CRIMES

One who was not so well enamored of Man of the Year Jack Walls was Cledis Hogan, a onetime enthusiastic Boy Scouts adult volunteer, whose son, Doug, had been intensively active in scouting. Cledis Hogan maintained to anyone that would listen that he and Doug had seen the other side of Jack Walls, and it wasn't pretty.

The feud had begun five years earlier, on Tuesday, December 29, 1992, when Doug Hogan, sixteen, joined other elite Order of the Arrow scouts for a wintertime camp-out. With the upcoming rugged jamboree camp-out at Boy Scouts campgrounds in Philmont, New Mexico, some of the scouts needed a reality check, a kind of shakedown cruise to prepare them for what veterans knew would be a challenging experience.

Doug Hogan was from Carlisle, a town neighboring Lonoke and similar in makeup and character, a farming community with at least twelve churches, a town where scouting was important. Scouting was important to young Hogan, too, who'd worked his way through the ranks, starting in third grade with Cub Scouts and continuing through into the Boy Scouts. He was now working toward earning his Eagle Scout badge.

Assistant Scoutmaster Jack Walls had sent word to Hogan to attend a camp-out at the Wallses' family farm, a site which had been donated to the scouts to use as a campground. Doug Hogan was reluctant. He liked Walls, but he didn't entirely trust him. He later said of Walls, "He loved to go camping, he loved the guys, he liked hanging out, having a good time. He worked real hard to be your friend, to get close to you." But he was leery of Walls. There was something off-putting about him that made Hogan uneasy.

His father, Cledis Hogan, shared a similar intuition of wrongness about Jack Walls, but there was nothing solid he could put a finger on. When Doug was about to go on his first trip to Philmont, New Mexico, with Walls's group, his father had asked him if he felt comfortable about it. Doug had said that he felt comfortable with it, and asked his father not to go.

But the Eagle Scout had picked up on a few cues floating around, such as the inappropriate way Walls sometimes spoke and acted with boys on camp-outs, telling one that he had "a nice butt" and playing a little grab-ass with him, wrestling around, stuff the other guys put up with.

Nothing definite, but enough for him to know that he didn't want to be alone with Jack Walls.

The camp-out would be a winter-type exercise to get the troop ready for Philmont. Walls specifically told Hogan not to bring along Chris Houchens, fifteen, who would also be going to Philmont. That was a bit odd, and Hogan didn't like it.

On the afternoon of December 29, Doug Hogan drove his pickup truck out to the Wallses' family farm campsite to drop off some gear, returning to Lonoke to pick up Chris Houchens and take him out to the camp.

Early the next day, at about six A.M., Hogan's pickup truck drove up to the McConnell home, dropping off Mark McConnell, fifteen, and his stepbrother, Keith Eaton McConnell, a few years younger. Grandmother Joann McConnell knew that the boys weren't due back until later that day. She knew by looking at their faces that something was wrong. Something had happened. She asked McConnell, "What's the matter, Mark?"

"Oh, nothing," he said, "it's nothing that should be talked about."

She said, "I want to know what's going on and what's the matter."

The previous night, most of the boys had retired to their tents by midnight, but Doug Hogan, Chris Houchens, another scout, and Jack Walls were still sitting around the campfire. Walls told the one boy to go to bed. A few minutes later, Houchens got up and went to his tent, leaving Walls alone with Hogan.

Earlier, Walls had passed around wine, letting the boys drink. It was against all the rules, and the law, but that was Jack for you. He treated a guy like an adult, not like a kid. What a great guy. Some of the kids got pretty drunk. Doug Hogan wasn't into it. When nobody was looking, he dumped his wine on the ground.

Now, Hogan lay down on his back near the fire. Walls came over, lying down beside him, in the opposite direction, his head down around Hogan's feet. He started talking to him about girls and sex, putting his hands on Hogan's legs.

Hogan later told *Court TV,* "I knew that was the moment that I had to stop it. And I felt that it was time to stand up very strongly and put him in his place."

Walls tried to unbuckle Hogan's belt. Hogan evaded him, saying that it wasn't his thing.

Walls said, "Well, if you won't jack me off, let me jack you off."

Hogan said, "That's not my thing, and you keep your hands off me." Hogan got up. Walls told him to go to bed.

Hogan later said, "I think he was shocked and then he got angry because he was afraid his secret was out."

Hogan went to his tent, waking Chris Houchens and telling him what had happened, that Jack Walls had been messing with him. Neither wanted to spend the rest of the night sleeping in a tent. They got up and made for Hogan's truck, which had an enclosed van-type box in the rear. They got in the back of the van. Outside, they could hear Walls moving back and forth from the truck to the campfire.

They knew that Walls carried a gun. It was contrary to all Boy Scout rules, specifically forbidden, but he did it all the same. He was a devout fire-arms fancier and shooter, a gunsmith and marksman. He had a gun, he'd been drinking, his advances had been rejected, and his secret revealed. They were afraid he might shoot them.

Hogan and Houchens got in the front cab, trying to start up the truck. Mark McConnell woke up and wandered over to see what was happening. Hogan told him. McConnell said, "Well, don't leave me out here." McConnell had been sleeping in a tent with his stepbrother, Keith, who continued to sleep through the night, unaware of what was going on.

Walls came over to the truck, told Hogan to shut off the motor, and asked him what he was doing and where he was going. He told them not to leave. Hogan would have been willing to try it anyway, except that he knew that farther down on the trail there was a water-filled pothole two feet deep, which had almost mired the truck earlier. He was afraid of risking the pothole in the dark, of getting stuck, and then having Walls coming upon him in the dark, gun in hand.

Walls wanted to talk, making a command

couched in the form of a suggestion that the trio come to the campfire. He told Hogan's companions his version of what had happened and asked them what they would have done in Hogan's place. McConnell said, "I don't know, I'd a' probably went berserk or something like that." Walls asked Chris Houchens what he would have done in Hogan's place. Houchens said he wasn't sure what he would do. Walls said, "Well, I was just playing, anyhow."

Hogan later said, "By the time he had come to me asking me to keep quiet, I'd already told two people. So then he had to talk about it and he wanted to convince all three of us that it was a big joke, he was just kidding, and that he wasn't really homosexual."

He and the other two decided to stay the night, sleeping in the pickup. At first light, joined by Keith Eaton McConnell, they started up the truck and got out of there, going to the McConnell house.

This was the first time that Joann McConnell had ever heard of such an accusation being leveled at Jack Walls. Upset, she said, "Now, somebody has to know about this." She called the Lonoke Police Department, who told her that since the incident had happened outside town limits, in the county area, she should call the sheriff's office. The dispatcher at the sheriff's office told her to notify the Arkansas Department of Human Services child abuse hot line.

Joann McConnell told *Court TV* that the woman on duty at the sheriff's department, told that the complaint involved Jack Walls, had said, "Oh, he's up to his old tricks again."

McConnell said, "What?"

"Oh, he's always acting funny."

McConnell didn't know how to take that. But she called the child abuse hot line to report what had happened, launching the first shot across the bows of officialdom. At the hotline, they asked if she'd mind giving them her name. She said, "No, I'm not afraid to give you my name." She told them what had happened, and they said they would investigate. They would contact the Lonoke Department of Human Services.

Court TV's interviewer asked McConnell what she would have done if Mark or Keith had come home to tell her that they'd been "messed with." She said, "I think I'd 'a' got me a gun and hunted him down and shot him myself. And I don't know anything about guns."

More seriously, she added, "I pray to God that none of it happened to my kids, but I always have a fear that it did, and they won't talk about it."

Ultimately, Mark McConnell and Keith Eaton McConnell both dropped out of scouting.

December 30, at six o'clock, early riser Cledis Hogan was sitting at home drinking his morning coffee, when he saw Doug's truck pull up into the driveway. He knew something was wrong, because normally the boys didn't leave a camp-out before noon.

Before he would tell his father what had happened, Doug Hogan made him promise not to do anything that would get him in trouble with the law. Cledis Hogan, not one to give his word lightly, gave his promise.

Doug told him about his camp-out night with Jack Walls. His father believed him. At first, he was so angry, Cledis Hogan said, "I wanted to kill Jack." But he'd given his word. After he settled down somewhat, he called Walls.

He recalled, "I did call Jack, and told him if he would get out of scouting, and get away from young kids, and not have anything else to do with them, that I wouldn't file charges. And he said he would."

Cledis Hogan told *Court TV,* "Most people really didn't know him that well. They knew his daughters, they knew his wife and his other relatives, but I don't really think anybody in Lonoke actually knew Jack. And that was the major way he got around without anybody saying anything, is that they had enough respect for his father and his position that they didn't want to see or hear anything else. They wanted him to be Mr. Good Guy."

Hogan received a call from Joann McConnell, who asked if his son, Doug, had talked to him. When he answered in the affirmative, she said,

"Good, because I have called the child abuse hotline. I made Mark tell me what happened last night."

"I'm so glad you did," he said. They talked for a while, both upset and unsure of what to do next.

On December 31, Cledis Hogan received from Jack Walls a letter of "apology," making no mention of what had actually happened at the campout, carefully phrased so that it might have been construed as an apology for not letting Doug Hogan leave the camp that night, for giving him wine, or for speaking harshly to him.

Part of the letter read, "I want to apologize to all of you for the incident at camp Tuesday night. It showed a flaw in my character that must be corrected and I must begin immediately. There is a great amount of trust placed in a man who works with young people as I did, and I violated it. I am ashamed of this as I have let everyone down from the Scouts through my own family. It's now up to me to change my life."

The first week of the new year found Cledis Hogan taking his complaint and Walls's letter to Jeffrie A. Herrmann, executive head of the Quapaw Area Council of the Boy Scouts of America in Little Rock, the chapter overseeing area scouting. Herrmann took the complaint seriously enough, on January 5 dismissing Walls as a volunteer scout leader—in other words, kicking him out. Walls appealed the decision, but his appeal was turned down. Privately, Walls took it hard, but publicly he kept the dismissal quiet, largely continuing his scouting activities.

The Boy Scouts also notified the Department of Human Services about the incident three separate times, including an agency hot-line notification on January 14, 1993. On January 19, Herrmann called the Department of Human Services Investigator Ken Murphy to discuss the case with him, following up with a letter stating that the Boy Scouts had found Hogan's accusations credible enough for them to sever Walls's connection with the organization, "terminating his volunteer status." Herrmann also enclosed a copy of Walls's letter to Cledis Hogan.

That's when the investigation ceased moving forward. For whatever reason, for the next 147 days, Murphy took no action in the case until May 26, 1993, when, prodded by a second hot-line report and Cledis Hogan's taking his complaint to Murphy's supervisor, Murphy finally initiated an investigation. He interviewed Cledis and Doug Hogan, then turned the investigation over to Lonoke County Prosecuting Attorney Larry Cook, who asked the state police to investigate.

In June 1993, Jack Walls attended the Philmont Scout Ranch in Cimarron, New Mexico, circumventing his being banned from scouting activities by registering as Joe Stocks, Heath Stocks's father. Heath Stocks was there, as were his mother and sister. Curiously, a photo exists from the gathering, a group shot in which Heather Stocks stands behind a seated Jack Walls, while Barbara Stocks is also in the scene. Did they know of the imposture, and if so, what did they think of it? The other scout leaders and campers seem to have said nothing about it. It's a puzzling incident never explained.

Except for some minor annoyances and inconveniences, Jack Walls's life continued as it had before the Hogan incident, running more or less smoothly and uninterruptedly. Friends and associates refused to believe that he'd done what he was accused of. They knew him—some had known him all their lives, all their children's lives. They trusted him with their children.

Also in June, with the investigation going nowhere, Cledis Hogan and his attorney met at the Lonoke Courthouse with Arkansas State Police Investigator James "Jim" Rainbolt. Hogan later said, "I don't think anybody believed us but my attorney." Asked why that was, Hogan replied, "Because nobody wanted to."

Rainbolt took a statement from Doug Hogan, who said that Walls had provided him with alcohol and sexually solicited him. Oddly, Rainbolt then classified the case as one not of sexual abuse, but rather of "false imprisonment," proceeding on that basis. Or, rather, not proceeding, since fifty-seven more days passed before he conducted his second interview in the case, this time with Jack Walls, who provided him with a written statement denying any wrongdoing or improprieties with Doug Hogan.

Cledis Hogan described it. "It said that Doug was lying. That Jack never did anything or said anything to indicate anything of that type. And that Doug was having problems dealing with girls. He placed all the blame on Doug."

Walls claimed that he'd chastised Hogan for his treatment of girls and "hit him on the belt buckle with the back of the hand," telling him to go to bed. His statement also explained away the December 31, 1992, letter of apology.

"Jack told them that it was because him and Doug had had words; and that he was too harsh with Doug in explaining to him that he shouldn't act the way he did, and all that, about girls. And the state police accepted it," Cledis Hogan said.

Three weeks later, with Hogan still complaining about the inaction, Rainbolt interviewed Mark McConnell and Chris Houchens, who both said that Walls had indeed admitted soliciting sex from Doug Hogan. Rainbolt did not interview anyone else who'd been at the campsite that night, or any other Boy Scouts or scout leaders.

Rainbolt told TV newsman Jack Vincent that he wasn't investigating a sex crime; he was investigating a claim of false imprisonment, namely, Walls's not letting Doug Hogan leave the campout that night. Vincent later opined that this was "the most botched investigation I've ever witnessed as a reporter in ten years. And it very well may've led to the deaths of three people [the Stockses]."

On October 8, 1993, Rainbolt closed his investigation, saying that Lonoke County Prosecutor Cook had "determined that the actions of the suspect in this case do not constitute a crime."

Such as it was, the investigation was stymied. The youth protection system was set up so that once a sex-abuse complaint came in, things were supposed to automatically start happening. But not this time. So far, there had been official mislabeling, misdirection, stalling, and obfuscation. Cledis Hogan thought he knew the reason why. Jack Walls was one of the town's most popular personalities, while his daddy, the Judge, was even more powerful. Judge Charles Walls, Jr.'s, picture hung on the Lonoke courtroom wall, along with pictures of other past and present jurists. Jack Walls had the clout and he was using it to derail the investigation.

Cledis Hogan refused to back off. He took his case to Pulaski County Circuit Court in Carlisle, where the Walls didn't have as much pull. On November 18, 1993, a judge signed two warrants against Jack Walls on charges of contributing to the delinquency of a minor and third-degree assault, both misdemeanors. On November 22, he was arrested on those charges.

The next day, the Department of Human Service's Ken Murphy wrote an official statement saying that after talking with Rainbolt and Jack Walls and others, he felt that "no sexual abuse took place or was intended." On November 30, someone filled out a form requesting the Department of Human Services's file on the case. The name on the form of the person making the request was, simply, "Walls." The request was granted, and a copy of the file issued to the petitioner. Such files were supposed to be strictly confidential, restricted to authorized agency personnel.

Jack Walls put out the word that Cledis Hogan was litigious, that he had what in local parlance was called "a name for suing people," although Hogan noted, "When we sued him originally, he did file a countersuit."

Doug Hogan came in for lots of abuse. People said he was a troublemaker, making it all up, and his family was using it to get their hands on some of the Walls money. They wondered why he didn't quit scouting, but he kept on with it, not backing off. It was a lonely time, a time to find out who his real friends were.

He recalled, "My friends were telling me, 'Quit making stuff up. You're a liar. You're gay. You're just making all this up to have a story. You just want to sue him and get some money out of him,' when that wasn't any part of it. It was all about getting him out of scouting and putting him in jail."

On April 8, 1994, a trial was held in the Carlisle courtroom, with Municipal Judge Gary Rogers presiding. The case was being prosecuted by one of Lonoke County Prosecutor Larry Cook's staff, representing plaintiff Doug Hogan, the same

Larry Cook who back in October had told State
Police Investigator Jim Rainbolt that he'd determined "that actions of the subject [Walls] in this
case do not constitute a crime."

Many area notables, including former state
Representative Bill I. Fletcher, testified as charac-
ter witness on behalf of Jack Walls. Members of
Boy Scout Troop #103 took the stand to refute
the charges, giving Walls a clean bill of health.
One of the witnesses was Heath Stocks.

Walls was found innocent of the charges. Now
that he'd been vindicated, his accuser Doug
Hogan was more of an outcast than ever. He and
his father both thought they were frequently being followed at this time, though nothing serious
ever came of it. Eventually, though, Jack Walls
wound up quietly paying the Hogan family a settlement. Cledis Hogan declined to say how much
it was, but informed sources reckoned it was
somewhere around twenty thousand dollars.

Angry, embittered, Doug Hogan quit scouting,
tearing off some of his hard-earned merit badges.
He told an interviewer, "Some of them, I took
off. But mainly, the ones that dealt with Jack."

The Knox family lived under a shadow. There
was a darkness there, a hollowness at the heart,
a gnawing wound.

It hadn't always been that way. Charles "Charlie" Knox sold real estate. His wife, Karen, taught
school. Married in 1972, they'd lived in Lonoke

ever since. They had a daughter and two sons, Brook and Wade. Charlie Knox's sister Pam was married to Jack Walls. Pam and Jack Walls and their three daughters lived across the street from the Knoxes, the two families sharing a common driveway. The Knoxes wanted to live close to the Wallses, so their kids could all grow up together. The two families went to church and Sunday school together.

Karen Knox told *Court TV,* "We shared our joys together, we shared our sorrows together." She felt that Pam Walls was like a sister to her, Jack Walls a brother. She described Walls as, "Wonderful. Caring. Compassionate. A wonderful uncle. I thought he loved my kids. I loved his. Charlie loved his kids."

They shared each other's lives, each always running over to the other's house. The Knoxes had it in their will that in the event of their deaths, their children's guardians would be the Wallses, and vice versa. To the Knox kids, they were Aunt Pam and Uncle Jack. Jack Walls got both boys started in scouting.

Brook was the oldest child, Wade the youngest. A change came over Brook around the time he was in the fifth or sixth grade. Until then, he'd been getting good grades in school and was popular, with lots of friends. Suddenly, for no discernible reason, his grades and friends both started dropping away. He withdrew from school activities, social contacts, becoming introverted, a loner. His parents couldn't understand why.

His mother thought the sparkle had gone out of him, the fun, the zest for life. She and Charlie were good parents, but they didn't know what to do. They spoke to Jack Walls—he was so good with kids, had such rapport with them. He said he'd be glad to talk to Brook. A day or two later, he told them that Brook was okay, that he was just going through some typical teenage changes, emotional ups and downs, "just trying to find his niche."

"He's happy, he's okay," Walls said. "It's just that he's just not into parents right now."

Karen Knox didn't like the sound of that. "Well, why shouldn't he be into parents? I love my child."

It wasn't that there were big problems with Brook. It was more like he was going through the motions, just existing. She'd ask, "Brook, is everything okay?"

He'd say, "Everything's okay. It's okay."

It wasn't okay. Not until he was in his senior year in high school did he once more begin to excel academically. Even then, he remained aloof, alienated, a loner.

Wade, the youngest, was dyslexic and had attention deficit disorder. He'd been in family counseling since he was nine years old. He had academic problems—he couldn't keep up with other students. Karen Knox could handle that. She was a teacher herself. But he also suffered from social problems: outbursts of anger, frustration, inability to fit in, running away from home, talk of suicide.

When he was in the fourth grade, he went to Little Rock's Elizabeth Mitchell Home, the Centers for Youth and Families, where he received daily counseling. He stayed there for a year, his mother and father visiting him two or three times a week, and calling every day. When his behavior was good, he was allowed to come home for the weekend. The only people authorized to check him out of the school were Charlie Knox and Jack Walls. When he came home on weekends, he would often go with the scouts on camping trips.

Karen Knox said, "We wanted our kids in the scouts, having wholesome good fun. . . . And it was a big deal in Lonoke to be in the scouts, and there was a lot of 'em."

Wade stayed at the center through the fourth grade, then came home. The stay seemed to have done him some good, at least for the two months that he was home before going back to school, entering the fifth grade. Then the problems started all over again.

The strain told on the family. Charlie and Karen Knox couldn't help but wonder if it was their fault. But if so, what had they done wrong? They watched their friends with their kids, doing the same things they did, only it was working. There was always turmoil in the Knox household. Their daughter was well-adjusted, a leader, but she didn't want to have friends over, because of the heavy atmosphere in the house.

Karen Knox recalled, "There was this thing in

my gut every day when I woke up, thinking: what is wrong? Something's not connecting here, something's not right."

There were years of trouble. She and her husband cut almost every social connection but church. They were ashamed. Their boys didn't function right. One was an introvert, a near-hermit. The other had mental problems and social problems. When husband and wife came home from work, they just wanted to hide. Which they did, for years at a time.

Neither Karen nor Charlie Knox had ever heard of Walls's getting caught for molestation back in 1969. Karen Knox insists, "I never heard anything about Jack. Never."

But they heard something about Jack in 1992, when Doug Hogan accused him of giving him alcohol and sexually soliciting him at the winter camp-out. It was crazy, it didn't make any sense, it was a nightmare. Why would anyone accuse Jack Walls of such things?

Walls said that it was because the Hogans were known for suing people. They were suing him to get some money. The Knoxes loved and trusted Jack and didn't know Cledis or Doug Hogan from Adam. Enraged by what they considered a scurrilous attack, Charlie and Karen Knox testified at the trial as character witnesses for Jack Walls, and the boys took the stand to tell what a great guy Uncle Jack was.

Still, there was that letter of apology which Walls had written to Cledis Hogan. Walls explained that he had written it for his family's sake, to protect them and settle things. He said he'd do anything to protect his family. The Knoxes could see some merit in his position.

Charlie Knox and Joe Stocks had been friends since boyhood days, going through school together, starting in the first grade. They'd joined the army under the buddy plan, going through basic training together. In later years, Charlie and Karen Knox and Joe and Barbara Stocks were very close friends. In the summer of 1996, the two couples had gone on a trip together. It seemed like they'd spent most of the trip talking about the problems they had with their kids, especially Heath and Wade. The Stockses were deeply concerned about their son, about the incredible rage he carried around with him at all times. He was out of control.

"Our problems were so similar," Karen Knox said, remembering. "Couldn't make 'em happy. No matter what you did, it was never right, it was never enough. There was no end to it."

During the Christmas break in 1992, Heath Stocks visited Jack Walls's house a couple of nights in a row, staying for hours at a time, until two or three o'clock in the morning, Karen Knox noticed. On or about the first Saturday in January 1993, Walls dropped over to the Knox house. Karen Knox was in the kitchen. Walls said, "I think Joe and Barbara are abusing Heath."

For once, Karen Knox's usual self-restraint failed her. She looked at Walls and said, "You are crazy, you are crazy. You know Joe and Barbara Stocks. You know what they've been through with that child. You know what they've tried to do for him. You know how much they've tried to help him. You know. And you tell me that they're abusing him?

"Jack, uh-uh. No. I'm not buying into that at all. Sure, maybe they haven't done everything right. But they are not abusing that child."

Walls uncharacteristically turned around, walked out of the kitchen, and out of the house.

The January 17, 1997, slaughter of the Stockses family hit the Knoxes like a hammer blow. Karen Knox heard the news from a neighbor: Joe and Barbara and Heather were dead and Heath was missing. She had a gut feeling that Heath had done it, and an equally strong feeling that if he had, he'd commit suicide. When she heard he'd been arrested, taken alive, she at first felt relieved, because she thought that meant that he hadn't done it after all.

But he had. Devastation set in.

When Heath Stocks was arrested, Wade Knox said, "No, he didn't do this. He couldn't've done it. He did not do this."

Summer 1997, was when things reached the boiling point. On July 28, at eight A.M., John Stanton, the Knoxes' next-door neighbor, drove up to

Charlie Knox's realty office. Stanton, weeping, said, "Jack has been molesting our son, Jim."

Knox said, "Why would Jim say that about Jack? What—what's going on here?"

"Jim has admitted that Jack has been molesting him for some time," Stanton said, "and . . . and . . . and he has Wade, also. You get Wade home and ask him."

Knox went home. He told his wife what had happened, what Stanton had said happened. He went into Wade's room, sat him down, and said, "Son, has Jack been molesting you?"

Wade said yes. The parents called their son Brook, attending college at Jonesboro. Charlie Knox said, "Brook, this is what happened. This is what we've learned. Is this true?"

Brook said, "Daddy, you believe every word those boys tell you."

So now the Knoxes knew that Brook had been molested, too. Charlie and Karen were numb, paralyzed. That night, at about eight-fifteen, they prepared to go next door to meet with the Stantons to decide what to do. Wade was taking a shower. It was getting dark outside. Jack Walls was standing out in his yard, watching. Watching them. That was something he seemed to do all the time. The couple had joked about it in the past. Now it wasn't so funny.

The Knoxes went over to the Stantons, huddling in the family room. They learned how the story had broken. Jim Stanton, sixteen, had told his parents that Walls had had sex with him, that he'd been having sex with him for years. The teen had broken his silence after seeing a camouflage jacket given to his younger brother by Walls. He knew that that was how the courtship started, with gifts. He knew because that was how Walls had started with him. He was determined to stop it before his kid brother was ensnared.

All four adults were dumbfounded, stupefied, at a loss as to what to do next. While they were hung up in indecision, someone else was taking action.

The doorbell rang. Ellen Stanton went to the door, opened it, and said, "Wade, Jack. Wade, you've got a gun, what's wrong?"

Through the doorway marched Jack Walls, with Wade Knox beside him, holding a gun to Walls's head. Wade had gone into his father's gun cabinet, taken out a gun, and used it to herd Walls into the Stanton house. Walls may have had good reason to believe that the teen gunman would not hesitate to shoot.

Wade said to Walls, "You go in there and you tell my mama and my daddy what you've been doing to me all these years."

Charlie Knox and John Stanton had already jumped up, moving toward the front door. Karen Knox stood stiff, afraid that Wade would kill Jack Walls, silently praying that he wouldn't. Charlie Knox said, "Wade, this is not the way—we can handle this. Give me the gun." Wade Knox gave him the gun, his father disarming it by removing the clip.

All the while, Walls had been standing there, wringing wet, "sweating like a hog," in Karen Knox's recollection.

Wade hit him, saying, "I said, you tell my mama and daddy what you've been doing to me all these years. You tell 'em how you've ruined my life."

Walls glared, hating, but he couldn't hold it. He slumped, the fight going out of him. He said, "It's true. It's all true."

There was silence. Dead silence.

Karen Knox told an interviewer, "Nothing about my life made any sense. . . . I just never could figure anything out. This is like living in a dark room, and you're just reaching out, trying to find a doorknob. Something to hang on to so you can open the door and maybe there's a light out there so that you can come out."

Now, the unknown had been made manifest; the unseen, visible. She said, "I knew in a flash, I knew in a second, what was wrong with my boys for all their life. I knew. I knew right then. . . . I had always looked up to him [Walls] and admired him. But when I looked at him this time, he had changed. He had changed forms visually to me. He looked like a monster standing there . . . so evil. He looked dirty, he looked filthy. He looked vile to me—it's like I could smell the evil on him."

Staring Walls down, she said, "You're the reason my boys are like they are. You sucked the life out of them, Jack. You deliberately, cold-heartedly connived it."

Walls just stood there, looking at her. For once,

he had nothing to say. Wade Knox ran out of the house, into the night.

Sometimes, things don't come apart all at once. The life they all had known—had thought they knew—was gone, but the new reality had yet to take shape. All were still in shock, including Walls. There was still hope that the whole filthy business could be handled quietly, that the boiling pot could be kept from bubbling over. It couldn't, of course, but that was the hope.

Charlie Knox talked about Walls's getting professional help. Walls said he would. Walls had to tell his wife, Pam, what had happened. That was one of the conditions, that he tell his wife. Walls left.

Pam Walls was away in Fayetteville, but after she returned, Walls didn't tell her. A day or two passed. Charlie Knox warned that if Walls didn't act, he would. Finally, on July 31, about nine in the morning, he and Karen called Pam Walls over to their house and broke the news. Jack Walls was away, at his job at Remington. His wife called him there, telling him to come home. She said, "I hope I never see him again. I hope he kills himself on the way home."

Walls came home, calling the Knoxes and telling them to come over. They went, knowing the risks. They were scared of Walls, with good reason. He was a gunsmith and marksman. He had guns and a reason to use them. He even had a key to the Knox house, from when the two families had been close, a few days ago, an eternity.

Having molested both his nephews, and the boy next-door, too, what act was inconceivable to Jack Walls, what wouldn't he shrink from?

As they walked over, hand in hand, Karen said to her husband, "If we don't make it out of here alive, I've loved my life with you."

He said, "Me, too, Karen. Me, too."

They met around the kitchen table, the Knoxes and Pam and Jack Walls. It was some meeting. At one point, Pam Walls allegedly said to her husband, "We can't continue to support you." What she knew about the extent of Walls's secret life is a matter of speculation, but it's probable that she wasn't entirely in the dark. Certainly she would have known about the Hogan lawsuit, with its hefty settlement.

The tense atmosphere around the table thickened to the point of choking when Karen Knox said, "Why did you rape my boys? Why mine, Jack?"

Walls said coldly, "I like the outdoorsy kind."

Events took another twist. Wade Knox had a long-standing appointment to see a psychologist, the appointment being scheduled for July 29, which came one day after the revelations. When the psychologists learned what had happened, they notified the Department of Human Services, as required by law.

The Department of Human Services called, investigating the complaint. Wade Knox made a statement. Jack Walls was arrested and held in jail, but that didn't ease the fear for Wade. He repeatedly told his parents, "You don't know Jack. You don't know the way he works. He'll kill us. He'll kill all of us." Walls had told him that in Vietnam, he'd seen people burned alive, he'd burned people alive, he liked to watch them pop, he liked the smell of burning flesh.

Wade Knox insisted, "You can have your house locked up, dead bolted. You can be in the shower, thinking you're by yourself. You can turn around in that shower, and Jack'll be in that shower with you, grinning at you. That's kinda the way he works. That's Jack."

Wade's parents learned that Walls used to sneak into Wade's bedroom at night, making his midnight creep, loosening the screen, climbing in through the window, crawling into the boy's bed, and raping him. In the morning, his parents would find the screen torn off the window and punish him for having done it. Now they knew better.

THE INVESTIGATION

Change was in the wind. The Lonoke Police Department's new police chief, Charles Peckat, hired on July 7, 1997, was just settling into his job when the Walls case came his way. Peckat was from outside the area, having spent twenty-one years as a police officer in North Little Rock. As an outsider, he was neither beholden to nor over-awed by the local power structure. He and

Lonoke Police Department Investigator Christopher L. Campbell began digging.

Peckat went to the Carlisle Courthouse to pick up a copy of the transcript of the proceedings of *Hogan* v. *Walls*, only to be told that Cledis Hogan had the only copy. Hogan brought it to Peckat, saying, "You don't really know what you've got into. You really don't."

Events in the case had taken on a momentum of their own. Initially, perhaps incredibly, the Knoxes and their neighbors were reluctant to prosecute, if only to spare their sons from having to testify, and for the sake of Pam Walls and her children. They wanted Walls to get treatment, but early in August, when they saw the "care-giving" Little Rock psychiatric clinic's diagnosis of him as a sex addict who could be "cured" in ten to twelve weekly sessions, it was insulting and infuriating. Pam Walls handed the diagnosis to Karen Knox, and said, "This is what they want Jack to do."

Karen Knox said, "This is ludicrous. This will never do. No."

Jack Walls still thought he could keep away from the law. He couldn't; the matter had been reported and the wheels were turning. He tried to contain the damage, minimize it into a small sentence, getting out on probation with no time served in the penitentiary.

As first Chief Peckat and then the state police began to investigate, more victims started coming forward, and the case became impossible to contain, despite the seeming efforts of some of the local power structure to do just that.

Prosecuting Attorney Larry Cook didn't want to prosecute, or even file charges. That put him on a collision course with Chief Peckat, who felt that the prosecutor was not proceeding properly, a feeling in which he was not alone.

The investigation that began in August 1997 stretched through to October 1 of that year, when police executed a search warrant on Walls's family house. The search combined elements of the Lonoke Police Department, state police, FBI and the Bureau of Alcohol, Tobacco and Firearms. The latter agency was interested in Jack Walls's formidable arsenal of firearms, not to mention allegedly having taught some of his boys how to make bombs and napalm. A quantity of explosive material was found in the shed where he kept his home shop.

Searchers also found stacks of pornography, a blond wig, notes prepping for the 1994 Carlisle Municipal Court case versus the Hogans, a copy of the state criminal code for sexual offenses, and a stolen gun. The porn, in books, magazines, and videos, included such material as *Female Animal, Boy Scout Mother, Scoutmaster's Wife,* and the ironically (under the circumstances) titled, *Confessions of Slippery Jack.*

On October 6, 1997, Prosecutor Larry Cook filed rape charges against Jack Walls on behalf of Wade and Brook Knox. The Lonoke Police Department and the Hogans requested that Walls be held in jail without bond. Larry Cook asked for $100,000 bond, which meant that $10,000 would have to be posted. This was swiftly done by Judge Junior Walls.

When the first charges were filed against Walls, Chief Peckat sat down beside Cledis Hogan in the courtroom, saying, "You remember what you told me the first time you met me? I didn't know. But I do know now."

Peckat was increasingly unhappy with some of the responses he was getting from Larry Cook. Peckat wrote a letter to Chancery Circuit Court Judge Lance Hanshaw, saying that the county prosecutor had questioned him as to whether it was wise to send the search evidence to the state crime lab. Furthermore, Cook was unhelpful in obtaining cooperation from the Boy Scouts, who were reluctant to turn over information they had gathered. He was resisting filing charges against Walls, having finally filed only two out of a possible seven separate rape charges.

Peckat's letter concluded, "The Lonoke Police Department has not received support, guidance, suggestions or communications from Larry Cook of the Prosecutor's office."

Judge Hanshaw was spared having to decide whether to remove the prosecutor from the case when Larry Cook recused himself, citing what he called a conflict caused by his having practiced law before Judge Walls, Jack Walls's father.

TV reporter Jack Vincent noted, "There were questions of why the prosecuting attorney that was handling the case originally didn't want to file charges, wanted to sweep it under the rug. There were a lot of rumors that were running around. But exchange of money was never one of the rumors. There were rumors that perhaps maybe he had been victimized himself at one point in time and didn't want it coming out."

He added, "It is the most sordid story I've ever covered."

Fearing local influence, the state went outside the community, appointing Betty Dickey of Pine Bluff as special prosecutor and Joye Cook (no relation to prosecutor Larry Cook) as victim witness coordinator. Betty Dickey was fresh off a case where she'd prosecuted a prominent south Arkansas attorney for bilking thirty-two clients out of their life savings. Now, she'd be tackling Jack Walls, the scion of a prominent east Arkansas family.

In early November 1997, she amended the charges against Walls to include six rape charges, two counts of violation of a minor in the first degree, and two counts of solicitation to commit murder. The latter two counts charged that Walls had instructed two of his favorites to kill Cledis and Doug Hogan. She also had Walls's bail raised to one million dollars, which he was unable to post. He was held in Lonoke jail.

The special prosecutor's investigation began in early October, gathering evidence and talking to

victims. Most of them initially denied that anything had happened. Dickey told *Court TV,* "Victims would first deny it, and we'd say, 'But we
know you were there with these three people and
they saw this happen between you and Jack.' And
they'd realize that we knew what had happened,
and they'd say, 'Yes, that happened, but there's
no way I'll ever take the stand and say that.' So
they were still, a lot of them, in denial, and a lot
of them couldn't emotionally handle it; who
didn't understand that facing it is a part of the
healing process. And they were still running from
it."

She added, "A further intimidation for the
children, even as they got older and were young
men was, they'd say to me, 'They'd believe him
instead of me. So that's why I didn't come forward.' Over and over again, they said they
couldn't fight that family."

Getting them to talk about it, even in confidence and privacy, was difficult, requiring tact,
empathy, and persistence. Sometimes it took
many hours to coax a story from a victim. This
was one of the responsibilities of Joye Cook. For
ten years, she'd been a victim witness coordinator
for the 11th West Judicial District prosecuting attorney, while for five years before that she'd been
a county rape crisis coordinator. A victim's advocate, she often worked with them from the outset
of a crime through the lengthy coils of the judicial process. She'd be with the Walls victims for
over two years.

Her task was simple, yet difficult to achieve: to win the victims' trust. She met with victims and family members during the day. Many nights, after official working hours, she and Special Prosecutor Betty Dickey would meet with victims in their homes. Joye Cook recalled, "Betty told them everything she possibly could. She didn't withhold information from them. They always felt like they'd been lied to, or that information was being withheld, critical information that they had a right to know. Betty took the view that victims do have a right to be informed, and to be treated with respect, and she did that."

Parents readily opened up. It was less easy for the teenage boys still harboring a lot of embarrassment, shame, and anger. When they started talking, though, the tales were of incredible, unbelievable things that went on, in some cases, for years and years.

Betty Dickey said, "It wasn't opening a file so much as opening a book. . . . We were looking at fifty to a hundred young boys over a period of maybe twenty to thirty years that he'd molested. At first, it's mind-boggling to think that you can handle a case that is so broad in scope. And then to try to control your emotions and look at it objectively was very difficult."

Even going back twenty-five and thirty years to the earliest victims, now grown men, the stories paralleled the most recent cases. Joye Cook observed, "Absolutely, the stories were the same. That's why we had no doubt that any of them were telling us the truth, because some of these men didn't even know these boys. And they were telling us the very same stories, over and over again."

Common themes emerged, patterns in Walls's technique. Joye Cook said, "He gave them alcohol, he gave them pornography. He would say things to them like, 'I'll teach you how to be with a girl.' And then he would have them . . . do horrible things to each other and to him. And then he would do these things to them. All in the guise of teaching them how to have a girlfriend."

Some of the boys he just used for fun and games. The special ones, the ones he chose, the more vulnerable ones, these were the ones he told, "I love you." These were the ones he severely abused. Some of his victims harbored mixed emotions about Walls, hating him for what he'd done, yet having believed for so many years that he was the only one who loved them.

Joye Cook said, "Some of these young men told us that they were afraid to tell because Jack had threatened them. He would show them his weapons and say, 'You know that I can do what I say I'll do.' He led them to believe that he was involved with other people that could take care of them. . . ."

Many victims were outside the statute of limitations. Once they were beyond the age of twenty-four, their cases could not be prosecuted. But even so, many of them had valuable information that could be used in the investigation and prosecution of the other crimes.

The final number was six. Six victims, six separate rape charges. Getting them to testify about it in the open would not be easy. Betty Dickey said, "To try to get the victims emotionally prepared for trial, besides getting them prepared to tell their story, was a challenge. Because these people, particularly the victims, were suicidal, and they were homicidal. They had been in trouble with the law, different ones. Their parents were devastated, and just overwhelmed with guilt that they hadn't known earlier. You're dealing with a fragile group."

Karen Knox agrees. "Jack had put these kids so far down anyway, that they could not look up and see the sky. He had humiliated them and controlled them. He had played mind games with these kids. 'Who would believe you? Look at you, look at me. Now, who'd believe you?' He said, 'People will think you're a liar. Besides that, they're gonna think you're queer.' Now, you hear that since you're eight years old or ten years old or twelve years old, when life is hard anyway, and you're trying to fit in and find your place. And then you hear that day after day after day. No, you don't fight back, you give in to it."

But the victims' days of giving in to it were just about over.

As the investigation progressed, a newly revised picture of Jack Walls emerged. In 1969, Walls, twenty-two, had invited a twelve-year-old Lonoke

boy to come over to his house. The boy had been
in scouting with Walls since he was seven. When
they were alone in the house, Walls took him up-
stairs, showed him some *Playboy* magazines, then
solicited him for sex. The boy turned him down
and got out of the house. He told his father, who
told Walls's employer, a farm-supply store owner,
who fired Walls. Not long after, Walls joined the
military and went to Vietnam.

That was the first known reported incident in
Jack Walls's child-molesting career, and the last,
until twenty-eight years later. Between those years,
Walls's estimated one hundred young male victims maintained an unbroken silence about what
had been done to them, keeping the secret from
parents, friends, and the authorities.

On returning home in 1972, Walls married
Pam Knox, started raising a family, and was active
as a volunteer scout leader. His first extensive
round of molestations began in 1976, with boys
in his troop whom he'd recruited into sexual service as members of what he termed his elite
"group."

Over the years, certain elements of his program
remained invariable, ironbound. One of the most
bizarre tactics was the "Betty" lure. He would tell
a boy or boys that once when he was young, a
woman named Betty had come into his kitchen
and seduced him. Now she had a hold on him,
using the threat of that liaison to blackmail him
into supplying her with fresh young lads for her
to perform oral sex on. Betty might call anytime,

and Jack's boys had to hold themselves ready to answer the call. When the call came, Jack summoned the boy or boys to his house, explaining the conditions. Betty didn't want her face seen, so the boy would have to be blindfolded. She mustn't be touched. Sometimes a boy's hands were tied above his head, to keep them out of the way. The boy would wait in the attic, blindfolded. Sometimes there were a couple of boys, all blindfolded, milling around.

Enter Betty. They could hear her, smell her. Her perfume reeked. They could feel her long hair brushing against their thighs as she knelt before them and orally copulated them. Only when she was long gone would Walls return to give the all clear, allowing the blindfold to be removed. When more than one boy was present, it was somehow understood without words that no one would speak of what had happened up in the attic. This suppression mechanism was at work in many of Walls's other group-sex forays.

When police finally searched Walls's house, one of the things they found was a blond wig. One boy, now a grown man, who'd been in the attic admitted that he'd peeked out from under the blindfold and seen that Betty was a perfume-drenched Jack Walls, wearing a wig and women's clothes.

Joye Cook said, "Most boys were embarrassed about their involvement in this. Some were very angry that he had scammed them like this. But you see why they never told. Who's going to tell that they allowed this man to take them up in his attic so a prostitute could come and have oral sex with them? Young men aren't going to tell that. That there might be several of them in the attic at once, all blindfolded at the same time. And when they left, they said they never discussed it among themselves."

For decades, Walls used the Betty lure, one of his most successful tactics. Perhaps Betty was not entirely bogus. During the 1980s and 1990s, an area woman engaged in group-sex parties with some of the boys and Walls.

After about ten years, the core group from the 1970s grew up and moved on, while Walls recruited a new generation of boys in the 1980s and 1990s. He began going after younger boys, some aged seven and eight. He was bolder, too, moving his sexual encounters from the family house attic to the living room, to the boys' homes, and to Boy Scouts camp-outs at the family farm. Most of the boys were members of the elite Order of the Arrow or Brotherhood.

To be initiated into the group meant having sex with Walls. There were circle jerks, oral sex on each other, and oral sex and sodomy with Walls.

How did he do it?

First of all, he had access. Access means opportunity. He had access to boys through his position in scouting, the vehicle he used to drive his secret life. Being a scoutmaster was a perfect cover, giving him a reason for spending large amounts of time with the objects of his desire, without attracting suspicion from parents and the authorities. As a scoutmaster, he was a kind of surrogate parent and authority figure. He was in a place where his interest and stewardship of the boys would excite only praise for his perceived altruism. He had them all to himself, in places where parents were absent, away from prying eyes, in intimate surroundings, camping out for long stretches of time.

Selectivity was another tool. Walls knew his prey. He picked on the most vulnerable—specifically boys with learning disabilities or family problems. They were easier. Psychologically, he offered acceptance, friendship, a mentor, "love."

Once chosen, the seduction program began. Here Walls had the advantage. He had something to offer, if only the seeming friendship of a "caring" adult, a sympathetic listener, someone who gave a damn, who communicated when parents couldn't or wouldn't. He'd spend hours with particular subjects, letting them talk their problems out.

Parents appreciated what they thought were Walls's attempts to reach out to youngsters. He could communicate where they couldn't. His reputation was such that they'd often ask Walls to intercede with their kids, figuring he could talk to them where they couldn't. When people had problems with their kids, Walls would volunteer to talk to them. Then he'd work against both sides, getting the boys in trouble with their parents and telling them that their parents hated them, that only he loved them.

Also, his "counseling" efforts gave him additional opportunities to pursue his agenda.

Courtship began with gifts. Adults have ready access to many things desired by the young. The forbidden fruit of guns, pornography, and alcohol were all used by Walls to break down the resistance of his young charges.

Guns helped provide an opening wedge. Karen Knox commented, "I know one of the boys said, 'After he let me shoot these real expensive guns, and taught me all this stuff, and took me all these places, and doted over me, he made me feel like I owed it to him. This is what I had to do. And that I owed it to him.' Mind manipulation, and control, and mind games. I know Wade was told, 'You just tell your mom and daddy exactly what they want to hear, and get 'em off your back.' And he learned that lesson well."

Pornography was a tool. A man who'd been one of Walls's original 1970s boys told of being taken out to the scout leader's family farm, for a fun day of shooting snakes. During a break, Walls took out a book and began reading aloud from it, a pornographic tale about a lad having sex with his sister. Walls suggested that his guest have sex with his sister.

With alcohol, he could get the boys to surrender. Once they'd participated, he had a hold on them, allowing the program to escalate. At best, to say no to Jack Walls meant alienating the affections of someone the victim often liked and admired, the man from whom good things flowed.

Submission seemed a small price to pay, when weighed against the benefits.

Walls used the classic behavioral stick and carrot of punishment and rewards. He was domineering. Fear was involved. He had guns and could shoot. He'd make a dangerous and frightening enemy. As Joye Cook said, "Some of these young men told us that they were afraid to tell because Jack had threatened them. He would show them his weapons and say, 'You know that I can do what I say I'll do.' He led them to believe that he was involved with other people that could take care of them. . . ."

He augmented his power and prestige by telling his boys "war stories" designed to showcase his potential frightfulness, almost boasting, "I've killed before, I've burned people alive."

What they did know was that Walls could hurt them, and that he'd make a bad enemy, possibly a deadly enemy to anyone foolish enough to lodge a complaint with parents, teachers or the law. Besides, who would believe the word of an accuser against that of the highly respected Man of the Year?

Doug Hogan's case proved that. As it turned out, all but one of the boys who testified in the Carlisle Courthouse about what a great guy Jack Walls was had been molested by him.

* * *

Heath Stocks's problems with his father made him ripe prey for Walls, who widened the gap between the two, working on Heath, aggravating their difficulties, telling him that his father and mother didn't love him. He did the same to his nephews, Brook and Wade Knox.

As Joye Cook said, "He's the most dangerous perp there is, because he can fool even his closest friends and relatives."

A final element working in Walls's favor was pure audacity. He who can think the unthinkable has an advantage over those whose minds work in more normal channels. Friends, family, and neighbors never suspected that the man they thought they knew was merely a cardboard cut-out persona, a role in a macabre masquerade. The idea that the Chamber of Commerce's Man of the Year, Judge Junior Walls's son, could rape and possess their young was simply beyond the pale—unthinkable.

As for the Doug Hogan story, those parents who'd heard of it didn't believe it had happened. They believed Walls was innocent, that it all sprang from some harmless misunderstanding that had been blown all out of proportion by the Hogans to squeeze some money out of Jack.

Joye Cook said, "Never did they believe that this man would do anything to harm their children. Or to betray them. That's why he's so dangerous."

* * *

One name that kept coming up in the investigation was Heath Stocks. An Arkansas State Police investigator phoned Stocks in prison and asked whether Walls had ever molested him. Stocks said no, but was somewhat more forthcoming later when Chief Peckat went to the prison and interviewed him.

After the Walls trial, in an exclusive interview with *Court TV,* Heath Stocks told the rest of the story about his relationship with Jack Walls, the events leading up to the family murders, and the killings themselves.

Like most of his school friends, Stocks entered scouting in the third grade, joining the Cub Scouts. That was fun and he liked it. The Boy Scouts were harder and he didn't like it so well. More than once, he tried to quit, but his parents wanted him to make Eagle Scout. He said, "Everybody wanted me to get Eagle Scout, follow through with it. Achieve a goal that people would recognize as something that took a lot of work. So they told me to finish up."

His parents trusted Jack Walls. Everybody's parents did. He was in and out of their homes, a neighbor to some, a relative to some, absolutely trusted with their children's lives.

How did Walls get to Stocks? What did Stocks get out of it that he couldn't get at home?

For starters, pornography and alcohol. Stocks said, "We were young guys, starting to get interested in girls. A lot of us don't have girlfriends, alcohol. Course we were young boys, so dirty pictures were always a good way to get everybody's attention."

More important, Walls provided a release from family pressures at home. Heath Stocks and his father didn't get along. Heath said Joe Stocks was a harsh disciplinarian. "His means of punishment . . . you wouldn't forget them for a week or so." Joe Stocks was a long-haul trucker, often away from the house for a week at a time. While he was away, Heath was supposed to be the man of the house, and when his father returned, the boy would be punished for where he'd failed to live up to that charge.

Stocks said, "I guess my dad had a lot of anger inside of him. Dad always wanted us to be the best of everything. So, when it wasn't the best, he tried to give me that little extra push. Just little things. No lying, no cheating, no stealing. That was always a biggie."

Stocks said that most of the other boys in Walls's group, his inner circle, had similar problems with fathers who had problems with anger, abusive fathers who made them feel unwanted and unloved at home. The vulnerable ones. Walls would move in on them.

"He made us feel comfortable, like a friend, at first," Stocks said. "The alcohol kind of loosed everybody's tongues. We talked about girls, we talked about life, talked about problems at home. Everything. So he knew about everything that was going on at home. All the parents trusted Jack. So if they were having problems with their children, they would talk to Jack. And Jack would talk to us. At times. Especially me. And I know that he talked to my parents a lot. Especially later on.

"And . . . and I didn't know it at the time, but he was telling me one thing, telling them another. Pushing us farther apart, so I'd draw closer to him."

So close, that there was a time when he called Walls his father. He called him Dad, and Walls called him son. "Stupid, now that I look back at it," Stocks said. "But after the years, it was all I had. I didn't know anything else to believe in."

He recalled the first time that Walls had come on to him sexually, at a camp-out in Damascus, a place where scouts from all over the state came to earn their merit badges. Walls gave alcohol to his group of boys. They were drinking and having a good time. One by one, the others drifted away into the darkness, finally leaving Stocks alone on a blanket with Walls.

Stocks said, "He performed oral sex on me, and then forced me to have oral sex on him. I was worried about it. I didn't know, really, what to say." At the time, he was ten years old.

The other guys came back. In any case, they hadn't gone far, just far enough away so that they could see without being seen. They congratulated Stocks, welcoming him to the group. A special elite group. His choice. His pick. The Group.

They'd all been through the same thing, every one of them.

He later heard that in some cases, Walls had threatened boys to keep them from telling, but he'd never needed to caution Stocks that way. Stocks was afraid to tell, afraid of what people would think. "I didn't want people saying I was a homosexual. For letting it go on for so long. That bothered me."

But Walls treated him the way Stocks wanted his father to treat him. Minus the sex, of course. Stocks didn't like the sexual abuse, but it was a trade-off. In return, he said, "I get treated the way I want to be treated. I feel loved, I feel needed. I'm not getting talked down to. Getting support, fatherly support.

"It was all a mind game, he played with our emotions. Played on our emotions. What was missing at home, he found out through our talks with him, and then he became those missing parts in our lives."

In high school, Stocks started dating a girl on whom he'd had a longtime crush. Walls warned him against forming any emotional attachments, urging Stocks to focus on having a sexual relationship: don't get close, don't get involved, love will hurt you. After six months, the girl broke off the relationship. Walls crowed, telling Stocks, "What'd I tell you? You wouldn't listen to me. What'd I tell you?"

Stocks said, "This thing that Jack called love, what he was doing to us, *that* he called love. When

I tried to find a real love, in a girlfriend or something of that nature, I always got crashed down. It didn't last. And it was like, it's not there. So I gave up on myself."

He didn't trust his family, either. "In my mind, sex was love. And my family didn't fit into that picture. So I pushed them away."

The sex at camp-outs continued until Stocks was an eighteen-year-old Eagle Scout. He continued to see Walls at his house through college, until his arrest. The sexual relationship tapered off when Stocks was in college. "He still tried to make moves at me from time to time. But Jack's interest was in younger boys, I do believe," he said.

Being part of the Group meant more than sex. Walls also used the lure of shooting big, expensive guns to bind the youths to him. Stocks said, "I think at first it was a means to keep everybody's attention. Here's military stuff—we're gonna blow stuff up and shoot weapons, automatic weapons, things of that nature. But as I got older, it turned into a protection. His little hit squad. Anybody tried to hurt Jack or, as he put it, take Jack away from us, we would defend him. With our lives, if necessary."

The interviewer said, "And you were willing to do that."

"Absolutely."

Attending college did not free Stocks from Walls's control. Walls told him who to date, what to wear on dates, what to do sexually with women.

After a date, Stocks would report back on it in explicit detail to Walls.

Stocks started dating a young woman at college. It started as a sexual relationship for him, then ripened into love. Walls felt threatened, and they had one of their first major disagreements. Walls suggested that Stocks "share" the girl with him. Stocks said no. Walls told him to break up with her. Stocks wouldn't listen. That's when Walls pitched the ultimatum: break up with her or kill her.

Stocks broke up with her.

He said, "I don't think a lot of people understand the things that this man did to us. I mean, he'd been in the military. A lot of it was, I think, based on military training: build you up, break you down, build you up, break you down.

"He was constantly pushing to see how much control he had. I'm not going to say their names, but I know that two brothers and a sister had a sexual orgy. It was Jack wants, Jack gets. Jack asks for, there's no questions asked, do as you're told. . . .

"Me, I don't like talking about it, and I've only brought it up a few times. For me, it was animals. An animal—not animals, but an animal."

The interviewer prompted, "Meaning . . . ?"

"Meaning that sick man made me do things with a dog," Stocks said. "It's not easy to talk about. At all. I mean, I can look back and go, God, what was I thinking? Why'd I let myself be put through that kind of stuff? And that all leads back to the same thing: love. The concept of love. I didn't know what it was."

Walls hated Cledis Hogan and his son, Doug, for bringing things out in the open and getting him officially kicked out of scouting. "As more pressure got on Jack, the more he hated Cledis and his son. He cost him his Boy Scouts," Stocks said.

Not that the ban had much cramped Walls's style. He was still having Boy Scouts camp-outs at the family farm as late as 1995. But once he'd been found not guilty in the Hogan case, Walls wanted revenge, offering to pay $150 to the first of his minions to catch up with Doug Hogan and hurt him. One of the teens gave Hogan a beating. According to Cledis Hogan, Walls paid a youth to beat up Doug Hogan, the attacker hitting Doug so hard that he broke his own wrist. The attacker's mother then had the gall to try to get Cledis Hogan to pay the bill.

Ego was involved, too. Walls felt that Doug Hogan had betrayed him by not accepting the role he'd been picked to play in the Group. He told the others, they're trying to hurt me, they're going to take me away from you all.

As time went on, and things heated up, Walls really wanted Cledis Hogan dead. Walls had been training his favorites in shooting and bomb making. Stocks said, "I know I was given a list of all the license plates of all the cars that he drove, familiar hangouts, places of that nature. Jack wanted us to catch up with him."

Cledis Hogan and Doug were followed by members of the Group. Once, Heath Stocks and two others were staked out outside the Hogan place, armed with a .45 and a silencer, intending to kill everyone in the house. The plan failed because they couldn't get the silencer to fit properly on the handgun.

But they never did catch up with Doug or Cledis Hogan and, after a while, the heat went out of the hunt and Walls moved on to other pursuits.

Events were coming to a head for the youth whom Walls boasted was his "finest creation." Heath Stocks was heading into a tailspin. He liked to drink. A lot. When he drank, he didn't care what other people thought. Sober, he worried about everything. He got drunk a lot. He flunked out of college. He got into trouble with the law on a DWI charge, followed by an arrest for making "terroristic threats" against a person he'd accused of stealing his motorcycle helmet.

What Stocks didn't know at the time, but only found out later, he said, after the murders, was that Barbara Stocks had found out about her son's relationship with Walls. Somehow, she'd managed to see them together in bed at the Stockses' house, without them being aware of her. She told her mother, Heath's other grandmother (not Dorothy Stocks, Joe Stocks's mother), and also told her minister. The grandmother later told Heath that Barbara Stocks didn't say anything because she was afraid Walls would hurt her family.

But the cat got out of the bag anyway, because Stocks said that he himself broke down and told his mother and sister what was happening, or at least enough of the picture to let the truth sink in. That happened about ten days before Friday, January 17, 1997, he said.

Whipsawed between two opposite poles, he then went and told Walls what he'd done. It was a reflex action to protect the master, done without thinking. Stocks said, "He lived my life for me, that's what it was. In my mind, it was a question of whether I could live without him. What could I do? I'd have to make my own decisions."

One of the maxims that Walls liked to drill into his Group favorites was, "If you have a problem, fix it. If you can't fix it, kill it." According to Stocks, when he told Walls that his mother knew, Walls said, "If you can't take care of the problem, kill it. I love you more than they do. And if you can't take care of the problem, you kill them."

Now, by telling the truth to his mother and sister, Stocks said, "I had created a problem. He told me to solve that problem."

The interviewer said, "And you knew what that meant."

"It was an order. No questions asked . . ."

"You didn't want to betray him."

"I wanted it to end, but he was all I had. And I was caught between a rock and a hard place."

On Friday, January 17, 1997, at a little past ten-thirty P.M., the problem was "fixed." Stocks described the immediate aftermath of the shooting

of his father, mother, and sister. "They're all
dead. They're all laying there. Just seeing him
[Joe Stocks], the years of the fighting, Jack saying
how much my dad hated me. He didn't love me.
I know that he had told me to kill the problem.
But in that moment I wasn't driving the car. I was
in charge when it wrecked."

The interviewer said, "And you didn't mean
for Heather to be killed in all this mess, obviously."

Stocks said, "I'd rather've killed myself than
murdering her or anybody."

". . . So you are solely responsible for these
three murders."

"That I know of. Yes."

"But you're not sure."

"I don't remember everything. I can't be
sure." But this he was sure of: "They didn't deserve to die. My sister and my mom, even my dad,
as many problems as we had had, he didn't deserve what happened."

After the arrest, Stocks was shell-shocked, an
emotional basket case. The first week he was in
jail, he went through detox for alcohol. He
couldn't eat, couldn't sleep, and lost about
twenty-five pounds.

Jack Walls was one of the first to visit him after
the arrest. Walls gloated, "I was right, you don't
have a conscience." He told Stocks to keep quiet,
that he was going to help him.

Stocks said, "It was weird. I get arrested; the
lawyer I have is best friends with Jack; the prose-

cutor is friends with Jack's father. The policeman that took the confessions was one of my dad's best friends.

"They wanted to get me down here so I'd shut up. I got three life sentences. . . . The prosecutor, he pushes the family, saying, 'I'll give him three life sentences; he doesn't take that, I'm going for the death penalty.' "

Stocks said his public defender lawyer told him that if he pled guilty, he'd draw a sentence of about seven years per life, that figured out to twenty-one years, he said. But when he went to prison, he saw inmates who were doing life sentences with parole, who'd already spent forty years in jail. In Arkansas, a life sentence with parole and life without parole could be pretty much the same thing.

While in the state hospital for observation, Stocks wrote a letter to Wade Knox, trying to help him. He knew that Knox had a lot of problems—and a lot of weapons. Charlie Knox came down to the prison to see Stocks, thanking him for the letter, saying it helped a lot. But he never got a response from Wade Knox.

The interviewer asked, "If you could say one thing to Jack Walls, what would you say to him?"

Stocks said, "I'd probably say, 'Why?' Of course, you know, I've now heard him say that he liked the outdoorsy types. That was his excuse. 'I like the outdoorsy types.' "

"Is Jack Walls totally responsible, in your eyes,

for making you pick up that gun and kill your family?"

"I can't blame Jack for me pulling the trigger. I can say that he was the cause of my mindset when it happened. The problems I had at that time, I can say that he was the major cause of those problems. But I take responsibility for what happened. And I realize that it was wrong. If I could take it back, I would. But I can't. That's reality."

The interviewer said, "We talked to two people yesterday who said what you said: Jack's going to get back out, but if he gets back, I'm going to kill him. Is that talk, or do you think he would last a day on the streets?"

Stocks thought that one over before answering. "Hmm . . . I think if somebody does kill him, that would be somebody that didn't step forward. A victim that never stepped forward. . . . If he gets back out . . . that'd drive Wade crazy. That'd drive a lot of those boys crazy. 'Cause the first thought that'd go into their mind is: he's going to get out and he's going to find us and kill us. He had kids hunting down other kids. Wade's scared to death of him."

"Anything else you want to say, after all we've talked about? Anything?"

"I would say that if there's kids out there and they are hiding a secret or they're being abused . . . don't let it go on. Stand up, do something about it. 'Cause I regret it every day, that I didn't. I really do."

* * *

One of the six victims Walls was charged with raping was Heath Stocks. Special Prosecutor Betty Dickey had him brought from prison to her office for an interview. Initially, he was sullen, uncommunicative, but he began opening up a bit during the first interview. But he didn't really come forward until late in the game, when the other victims had already given their statements and Jack Walls neared a conviction.

Betty Dickey said, "This is a young man who, when he was ten or less, was befriended by a person who sexually abused him, but a person who he loved, and who loved him, and in whom he trusted. Whom he exchanged that parental relationship for. And so he wasn't going to easily give that up, because I think Jack apparently told him he'd take care of him. Jack not only told him to kill his parents, we firmly believe, we're not so sure that Jack didn't participate in the killings."

Had Walls influenced Stocks to kill his family?

"I'm not absolutely convinced, not convinced beyond a reasonable doubt," Dickey said. But she pointed out Walls's statement to Stocks. "If you have a problem, take care of it; if you can't take care of it, kill it." Heath Stocks's mother knew of the relationship with Walls.

Dickey said, "We believe that Jack told Heath to kill his parents and his sister."

Corroborating this was what Barbara Stocks had told her minister and mother about a week before she was killed. Dickey said, "She apparently confronted Heath about the relationship and he was enraged. Both the sister, mother, and father were frightened of Heath. She had two conversations with the minister just before she was killed."

This contradicts Stocks's interview statements, where he said he didn't know that his mother had found out, and that he told her and Heather. In Dickey's version, he's "enraged" when Barbara Stocks confronts him, a somewhat different scenario.

This development came when Heath Stocks's maternal grandmother, Barbara Stocks's mother, was asked by the special prosecutor's office if she wanted to testify in the penalty phase. She volunteered that Barbara Stocks had told her a week before she was killed that she knew about the relationship. This fine-tuned the motive: Barbara Stocks had learned her son was having sex with Jack Walls, she confronted him about it, he told Walls that she knew, Walls told him to get rid of her.

This was the first that Dickey and her team had heard of it and the information came only a week before they were slated to go to trial. When asked why she hadn't come forward earlier, the elderly woman revealed a confused misunderstanding of the judge's gag order, wrongly believing that she'd been bound by the order prohibiting attorneys from talking about the case to the press.

Why did Stocks tell Walls that his mother and

sister knew? Dickey believed it was because Walls was Stocks's substitute father. It was classic pedophile technique, to control the victim's mind and program him. She said, "That is part of what a pedophile does. They brainwash them into believing you're their best friend, they love you, your parents don't love you. They treat you like an adult because they give you alcohol. They talk to you about sex. They show you porno videos—Jack showed them trashy porno magazines that involved Boy Scouts. And did every perverted act you can imagine to and with these children. It's just unbelievable, what he got away with."

She tried not to get involved in the Stocks family murders case file and photos. "Because our responsibility in this case was to look at Heath as a victim. And not as the perpetrator . . . Heath Stocks was a victim in our case. Heath Stocks committed three brutal murders. And he will tell you he bears a whole lot of the responsibility. To understand how an adult can take a child's mind and twist it into something like Heath became, and then have it kill for that adult, is something that someone needs to take an objective look at. But my job was to look at Heath as a victim. And as I said, I never chose to look at the pictures of the brutal murders that Heath committed. Because my job was to prosecute that rape case, when he was a victim.

"So I'm saying someone needs to look at it."

She learned that Barbara Stocks had also spoken to the minister of her church about Walls's involvement with her son. The minister didn't want to talk, saying he was trying to hold together a church which had been devastated by the murders, and his congregation didn't want him to get involved. His duty was to the church, to his flock, and to helping them heal emotionally. Dickey reminded him that he had a duty to tell the truth. He felt that what Stocks had told him was a privileged communication. Barbara Stocks had told him in confidence. Now, from his prison cell, Heath Stocks released him from the bond of silence.

The minister still didn't want to get involved. Dickey did some arm twisting, pointing out that if Walls was not sentenced "appropriately," he'd be tried for murder in the Stocks family deaths, the minister would be subpoenaed, and he'd have to testify anyway. The minister later testified during the trial's penalty phase with the permission of his congregation, his church's district supervisor, and its bishop.

THE TRIAL

For the defense, the Walls family engaged Hubert Alexander of Jacksonville, who brought attorney Jon Johnson into the case. When the legal firm with which Johnson was associated first took on Jack Walls as a client, only two rape charges had been filed against him. Things soon suffered a domino effect, with the charges climbing up to six victims when Johnson first got on the case. Once Johnson joined, he discovered that there could be as many as fifty different victims, or more. But Walls was only charged with raping six.

During the pretrial period, the prosecution and defense jockeyed for position, jousting. Providing leverage for the state was the solicitation to commit murder against the Hogans charge. Other tools came to hand, upping the pressure on the defendant. Betty Dickey learned that Walls was transferring property to his wife, whom he was in the process of divorcing, in order to show that he was indigent and therefore eligible for a public defender to represent him. If he didn't use his money but the taxpayers' to subsidize his defense, the trials could potentially drag on for years.

Dickey examined the real-estate records showing the transfers of property, scrutinized the couple's assets, and subpoenaed documents that showed that Walls was attempting to perpetrate a fraud on the court. With that route blocked, Walls would have to use his own money to pay his lawyers, putting financial pressure on him to cop a plea to keep from depleting family financial resources.

On the conspiracy to commit murder charges, Cledis and Doug Hogan knew that if they pressed charges against Walls, they'd also have to prosecute the boys involved, Wade Knox and Heath Stocks, which they didn't want to do, if they could avoid it. They told the prosecutor that if Walls would plead guilty to the sex charges, they would withdraw the conspiracy to commit murder charges.

Walls made his bargain on January 6, 1998, agreeing to plead guilty to five of the rape charges. He would not plead guilty to the rape of Heath Stocks. The prosecution believed his reluctance to admit to the Stocks rape was because it would put him one step closer to the Stocks family murders and a possible murder charge. Walls dug in his heels, not budging. On the eve of the trial, Betty Dickey arranged for both Stocks and Walls to be given polygraph tests. Heath Stocks passed the test and Jack Walls failed it. Walls agreed to plead no contest to the charge of raping Heath Stocks.

Before, during, and after the trial, Special Prosecutor Betty Dickey never had the opportunity to question Walls.

January 22, 1998, was the day of the victim impact statements. Here was an emotion-drenched, marathon encounter session, pierced by sorrow and rage: sorrow at the lives that had been emotionally stunted, warped; and rage at the man who'd violated their trust to turn them into his sexual chattels.

Now Jack Walls beheld his ultimate legacy. The six victims whose rapes he had been charged with took the stand, one by one, to confront him with what he'd done. Most had first been molested by Walls at around age twelve, with the oral sex and sodomy continuing anywhere from a few months to a number of years. They told of the aftereffects haunting them even today: a lifelong fear of intimacy, the inability to trust, job loss, alcoholism, drug abuse, trouble with the law. Beyond what had been done to them lay the ripple effect, the ever-expanding outward wave of disturbances, stresses, and strains inflicted on families over the years. The families' not knowing that the reason for the behavioral and social problems plaguing their troubled sons was that they were in sexual and psychological thrall to Jack Walls.

Wade Knox told of the July night in 1997, when he'd gone next door to Jack Walls's house and held a gun to his head, saying, "Come on, you're going with me. You're gonna tell my parents how you've screwed up my life."

According to the witness, Walls said, "If you bring me down, I'll bring you and everybody else down around me."

Knox said, "I'll have to take that chance, but right now you're gonna go with me and tell my parents how you screwed up my life."

He and, later, Heath Stocks both testified that Walls had asked them to kill Cledis and Doug Hogan, and that they'd stalked them both. The last of the victims to testify was Stocks, allowing him to hear the stories of the other victims who took the stand, stories which differed only in duration and degree from his own personal experience with Jack Walls. He said that Walls had been his friend, his mentor, his god. He still loved him, he said. He would have done anything in the world for him.

Walls had trained him to be an assassin, a conscienceless commando-style killer. Walls had always told him, "If you have a problem, fix it. If you can't fix it, kill it." Barbara and Heather Stocks's knowledge of Heath's relationship with Walls was a problem. Heath had made it and it was up to him to fix it. Walls told him to kill his family.

The initially reluctant witness, the Stocks family minister, Reverend Robert Marble of Concord Methodist Church, testified that Barbara Stocks had told him twice that she knew of Heath's sexual relationship with Jack Walls. On January 8, 1997, she told Marble, "We need to talk." Nine days later, before they could have that talk, she was dead, slain by her son.

Marble said that he'd seen Heath Stocks twice after his arrest, once in jail and once in the Little Rock State Hospital, where he was undergoing psychiatric evaluation. "When I asked him why, he said, 'Jack told me to do it' on both occasions . . . to kill his family."

The witness said that he hadn't come forward with the information before now because he believed that his conversations with Barbara Stocks were privileged communications between a church member and her clergyman.

On February 5, 1998, before handing down

Walls's sentence, Judge Lance Hanshaw noted that a few, very few, people had written him urging him to impose a light sentence. Scornfully and with ringing old-fashioned rhetoric addressing the defendant, he thundered, "None of those people were present on January 22 to hear the anguishing testimony of some of those violated by you. They will never read of the pornographic filth plied to your young victims to arouse them, or know of the various alcoholic concoctions created to dull their senses and to loosen their inhibitions, or of bringing certain women for sexual activity so you could reap the rewards of satisfying your pedophilic mind.

"They will never know of the vast amount of time you must have spent conjuring the various lurid schemes to entice one or several young men into your self-centered web. Only a few truly know the depth of your unfaithfulness.

"Many young men, for whom you were not charged because of the statute of limitations, have cried and wondered for years why these things happened to them.

"After reading the files and seeing the names of many whom you have violated, it takes more than one hand to count those that I personally have jailed and sent to prison. When we count the costs of your actions, directly or indirectly, the cost is staggering."

He'd come under plenty of pressure about the case, the judge said. "I will say that none of the victims and no one from the defendant's family pressured me. There was a lot of pressure in this case, but I made up my own mind."

Addressing the grievances of the Hogan family, Judge Hanshaw said, "I do not have to believe Doug Hogan's story that you attempted to unbuckle his pants, to know that you have caused others to ridicule the Hogans and attempt to make them less than they are in the eyes of the public, and that many of these young men stalked the Hogans for you."

In conclusion, Hanshaw said, "I do not have to believe Heath Stocks's testimony to know that he was your finest creation, and perhaps most vulnerable victim, and to know that he became what you taught him to be. I only know that, in the very least, you are indirectly responsible for the deaths of Joe, Barbara, and Heather Stocks."

Jack Walls made a statement in court, apologizing to the victims and their families. "At this time, words of apology would ring somewhat hollow, but I wish there was something I could do or say to these victims and my family that would somehow relieve some of the pain and suffering I've done. I wish that there had been something or some kind of help for people like me before the fact instead of always after." As always, it was still all about him.

Cledis Hogan told an interviewer, "You would've had to have seen him through all these court procedures in Lonoke. Until the day they sentenced him, not the day that he pled guilty, but all the way to the day that they sentenced him, he was so arrogant; he thought Daddy was gonna come riding in on a white horse and rescue him."

Post-trial, Lonoke Police Department Chief Charles Peckat said he would have liked to reopen the Stocks murders to investigate Jack Walls's possible involvement, but the crimes had been committed outside his jurisdiction, hamstringing his ability to follow up. The crimes fell in the bailiwick of Lonoke County Sheriff Charlie Martin, who said that it was Heath Stocks's word against Walls's, and that he'd seen no evidence that would convince him to reopen the case.

Originally, Judge Hanshaw had sentenced Walls to four life terms, to be served consecutively. Plus two forty-year terms, to be served consecutively. On March 4, 1998, the state supreme court overturned on appeal Walls's sentence of four life terms and two forty-year terms.

Walls's attorney, Jon Johnson, told *Court TV*, "Basically, he had no prayer whatsoever to get out of prison. We appealed that decision based on the testimony that was of Heath Stocks in the murdering of his parents and sister. That was allowed in. We appealed on that issue, and the supreme court reversed the decision because of the testimony concerning the death of his parents and sister."

The testimony was Stocks's accusation that Walls had told him to kill them. But Walls wasn't on trial for that—he was being sentenced for rape, not murder. Johnson successfully argued that the evidence was irrelevant, considering the sentencing purpose. "His second sentence was basically, he got three life sentences, but they ran concurrently, which means that he's got one life sentence. . . . So basically, in legal terms, he got one life, plus forty years, instead of four lifes plus eighty, which is what his last one was.

"It's a huge drop, but in Arkansas, pretty much, life is life, and the chances of him getting out are very, very, very slim. In fact, there may not even be a chance. . . . And even though the sentence is a lot less, we still have to try to do our job." Which meant filing a second appeal.

The interviewer said, "A lot of people that we've talked to, the first thing they say is, 'Well, Jack got a drop in sentence, and we know he's gonna get out. There's no doubt in our mind he's gonna get out.' "

Johnson said, "I—I understand their concern. But it's my legal opinion—and they might not value that very much at all—that I don't think he will get out, with a life sentence. You might get some lawyers to say that he may have a chance to get out. I mean, it's been my experience from what I know that he won't."

He added, "My job was basically to help defend Jack Walls to the best of my ability—which is what I'm trying to do, and a lot of people don't understand that. This is the profession I chose to be in, so I understand that."

What was Walls's reputation in the town before the arrest?

Johnson said, "Well, he's a family man, has three daughters, a loving wife, works in the community, a scout leader. His father was a chancery judge, well-respected man in the community. So by all accounts, from my information, it was a good reputation he had. I've never—and I'll be honest with you—I've never asked him, 'Jack, tell me, did you do this or did you not do it?'

"That can affect your ability to represent somebody on a case, if he admits to you that he did do these things."

He was asked, "What made Walls admit to all this? What was the thing that really did it?"

"I'm not sure," Johnson said. "Sometimes it may be the pressure of putting the children through the trial process. I mean, people need to understand that we could've made the state go through the trial. And that would've pretty much forced the state to call every one of those children to testify about every detail that happened to them."

The interviewer pointed out, "Well, they still had to do that."

"We could've gone through the whole trial process of that. Which means make them prove every element of the offense. But as far as what made him go ahead and plead, I—I don't know."

Johnson said that when he visits his client in prison, Walls's first concern is to ask how his kids are doing (his own daughters). "He's really scared, himself, in there, you know, being in prison, the stories you hear about the people accused of or convicted of child molestation, and you know, some of those are probably true."

The interviewer said, "He's afraid for his life?"

"Yeah."

"What is a fair sentence for Jack Walls?"

"Are you asking me as his lawyer, or as somebody who might have a kid—are you asking me as a lawyer or as a parent? As a parent, you probably couldn't put him in there long enough, you know, if he's convicted of doing these things, and it's my child," Johnson said. "As his defense attorney, we're trying to do the best we can for him. We hope that he'll be able to get out someday. . . . I think that's our job as defense counsel, to do that. People may not understand that, either, but . . . I think that's our goal, is to allow him to have a chance to get out. I mean, we can't be his defense lawyer and tell you that we think it's fair for him to be locked up forever."

The interviewer asked, "Do you think it's possible that you can control a person's mind, to such an extent, where you can drive someone to kill, because somebody says, 'If you have a problem, kill it'?"

Johnson said, "Jack Walls denies telling him [Heath Stocks] that to begin with."

"Denies telling him what?"

"Telling him that if you have a problem, kill it—or anything resembling that."

"Ever? In the whole time he's known Heath Stocks?"

"I don't believe I can tell you that, yeah." Johnson noted that of the fifty or so alleged victims who'd come forward, only Heath Stocks had killed his parents.

The interviewer said, "Does Walls also deny that he controlled his life, that he told him who to date, how to dress, what kind of sex to have, to break up with his girlfriend? Does he deny all that?"

"Yeah, I think he denies all that," Johnson said. "When he pled to the crimes, the only one he didn't plead guilty to was the Heath Stocks rape. And that's the one he pled no contest to."

"Is that because he thought he'd be linked with the murders?"

"That's a tough one to answer. I don't know about that."

"Okay," the interviewer said. "Another question I have is, didn't you find it curious that Jack Walls was house-sitting the Stockses' house days after the murder?"

Johnson said, "It depends on what you think their relationship is. If you think their relationship is he was concerned about the situation, and that's basically it, he was a friend. I mean, it would not be unusual for a friend or somebody who they looked up to to do that."

"Is it possible he was in there looking for maybe incriminating evidence?"

"Well, I don't know."

Wrapping up, Jon Johnson said thoughtfully, "I've been asked by people, 'How can you defend a guy like this?' It's hard to answer sometimes. As I say, I think it's an obligation. . . . I feel obligated to at least, the best I can, to defend Jack Walls on some of the issues.

"I mean, I can close by saying I'm like everyone else. I hope there is a resolution to this very soon."

More trial aftershocks followed. In October 1998, the Department of Human Services's Department of Children and Family Services opened an internal investigation headed by attorney Lloyd Warford, probing the way that the agency had handled, or mishandled, the Doug Hogan case.

Among Warford's findings was that when Joann McConnell complained on the department's child abuse hot line, the internal hot line report described the incident thusly: "Scout leader tried to get the boy drunk and tried to get the boy's pants off. Scout leader gave the boy several drinks of wine." At that time, the report went to Department Investigator Ken Murphy, working in Lonoke Department of Children and Family Services. Somewhere along the line, the hot-line allegation was classified not as "sexual abuse," but as merely "abuse."

Warford noted that the difference in wording was important, since they indicated two different administrative levels of complaints. Department rules mandated that a "sexual abuse" case must be immediately reported to law enforcement. But an "abuse" allegation would be referred to the local Department of Children and Family Services office for investigation.

Jeffrie A. Herrmann of the Quapaw Boy Scouts council had notified Murphy of the complaint four different times, reporting that the scouts had terminated Walls's association with the organization and enclosing a copy of the apology letter. In such cases, the law required Murphy to initiate an investigation within 72 hours of notification, and to complete the investigation within 30 days. Murphy took no action for 147 days, when he finally began an investigation that was, at best, desultory.

Then there was the report written by Murphy on November 23, 1993, one day after Jack Walls's arrest on misdemeanor charges of contributing to the delinquency of a minor and third-degree assault. Murphy's report read, "Mr. Walls had a reasonable explanation of the events that supposedly took place and the police investigator that interviewed him and others also feel that no sexual abuse took place or was intended." Also, it was learned that Walls had considered calling Murphy as one of his witnesses at the Hogan trial, but changed his mind.

In March 1999, the Department of Children and Family Services fired Murphy.

An Arkansas State Police spokesman refused to

comment on their handling of the Hogan case until all the court cases involving Jack Walls had been resolved through the appeals process, saying that discussing them could impact the litigation.

Summing up, Betty Dickey said, "This is a wake-up call for parents to understand that nobody should ever be a better friend to your child than you. And anybody who tries is suspect. Whether it's a Boy Scouts' leader, whether it's a church youth minister, whether it's a football coach. Nobody should be a closer friend to your child than you. And anyone who is, especially who is at the expense of his own family, like Jack was—Jack has three daughters, he spent more time with these boys, apparently, than with his own family. I mean, that ought to be a wake-up call for a parent. You know: why's this guy spending more time with my child than his?"

She added, "If we could've asked for the death penalty for Jack Walls, we would've. That was not an option. But Jack didn't just take their childhood and destroy their innocence; he replaced it with a sense of shame and guilt and fear. . . . So he has destroyed so many families' lives because of what he did, that he doesn't deserve to live."

The ripple effect: each violation sent shock waves through not only the victim, but the victim's family, friends, and neighbors. Many of Walls's victims have marital and relationship problems, divorces, substance-abuse problems. Some have served time in the penitentiary for drug offenses. They can't hold jobs, have a lack of trust and a fear of intimacy.

Victims' advocate Joye Cook noted, "So many of them are still going through horrible devastation in their everyday life. They just can't cope, can't get past it.

"Jack Walls has to be the most evil man that I have ever come across in any case I've ever dealt with. And the devastation he has wrought on so many families is incredible."

"Jack Walls affected a lot of kids here," Lonoke County Sheriff Charlie Martin said, "but the fact remains that none of these kids killed their family. Heath Stocks is the only one that killed his family. Jack Walls, I think, is right where he needs to be. Heath Stocks is right where he needs to be. Basically, I hope that neither one of them sees the light of day again. They spend the rest of their life there. And that's hard for me to say about Heath Stocks, because [of] the association I had with Heath Stocks and Barbara and Joe and Heather. It's hard for me to say that. But . . . I think he's right where he needs to be."

He said that when he talked to Stocks, the only sign of remorse he showed, and then not much, just a tiny flicker, was when he asked him about Heather. "Because even now, I can't understand why Heather, why he killed Heather. Heather always took up for Heath. And she always looked out for Heath. She was calling us to tell us that somebody burglarized the place. To take the heat off of Heath whenever Joe and Barbara came in. She was still looking out for Heath."

Which brings up the question: if Heath Stocks didn't kill Heather, who did?

Early on, there were rumors that Heath Stocks hadn't been alone at the crime scene. Sheriff Martin investigated those rumors, but no hard evidence was ever found to back them up.

One version had Jack Walls present, but not participating at the scene; another had him watching the house from inside a parked car on the street. Betty Dickey was asked by an interviewer, "You think there's a possibility that Jack might've also been there?"

She said, "There's a good possibility that Jack was there. That's not something we can prove, but we have every indication that he not only told him to do it, but he was there to see that it was done, if not participate in it. And then Jack was the one everybody turned to to secure the scene after the murder. And Jack was the one who kept going around asking the other people involved, 'Did Heath say anything else?' "

During Heath Stocks's *Court TV* interview, he was asked, "Was anybody else in that house with you that night?"

Stocks said, "Not that I can remember. There wasn't anybody that I saw when I left, I can tell you that. I know that there's somebody who has said that they were there at the house when it happened, that Jack was within a short distance away in a car. It was one of the other boys. And he said that. . . . Said they watched. And that same boy, after I was locked up, he was given a gun, told to kill his family. And turned the gun on Jack. Made him go confess."

Stocks finished, "As far as I know, nobody else was there."

Whoever was at the house that night, it's a fact that Stocks wore gloves during the killings, and took some jewelry away with him. Arkadelphia investigators later recovered the items. Add that to the way the house was ransacked, dresser drawers upended, their contents dumped on the floor, it could be argued that Stocks was trying to make it look like Joe, Barbara, and Heather Stocks had surprised a burglar, who had panicked and gunned down all three. This indicates premeditation, rather than the unthinking "saw his father and started blasting" scenario which was a centerpiece of Stocks's account of the murders. The discrepancies in Stocks's account must be taken into consideration when weighing his credibility.

Joann McConnell, who in 1992 had made the original complaint to the child abuse hot line about Walls soliciting Doug Hogan for sex, was asked, "Why do you think it took so long to get Walls behind bars?"

She said, "Because nobody wanted to believe it. The type of family he comes from, he could buy his way out of it. His father is a judge, and they own half of downtown Lonoke. You know, money talks anywhere. They tried to cover it up. He bought his way out of it."

Describing Lonoke, she said of the citizens, "Most of 'em are good people and religious people. But there's a lot of snakes here, too."

Her husband, retired police officer Lucien McConnell, added, "Everybody liked Jack. *I* liked Jack. There's a lotta people here that think he's innocent as a newborn babe. Even after he admitted it."

Doug Hogan told *Court TV,* "Some see me as the guy who came forward first and told the truth in the beginning. Some see me as the guy that would keep his mouth shut and just let it go. I thought he [Walls] truly loved boy scouting and the way that boy scouting was, and what it meant to him."

The interviewer said, "What do you think it meant to him now?"

"It was a tool that he used to get boys."

Cledis Hogan was asked, "Say Jack Walls gets out—what will you do?"

"Kill him," Hogan said.

The questioner said, "No doubt in your mind that you'd do that."

"No doubt in my mind," Hogan said. "I'll have to. He still has a power over my family. And if I don't kill him, my son will."

"Even if you may have to go to jail the rest of your life."

"I'd rather my life than my son's."

"Do you think if Jack Walls gets out, he'll come after you?"

"Very possible. But the worst part is he may come after my son. Or hurt some other member of my family. I can't take that chance."

Cledis Hogan believes that Heath Stocks killed his parents, but that someone else killed Heather; that Jack Walls was there, but that he didn't directly participate in the killing; and that a third party, whom he doesn't care to name, killed Heather Stocks.

Hogan said, "My family's fortunate. We didn't lose any member of our family. Jack didn't actually molest Doug. He put the fear in him for about five or six hours that he was gonna lose his life. And of course, looking back now, I can see that Jack wouldn't necessarily had to have been the one to kill Doug. He had enough people there at that camp that night.

"There were people that thought Doug lied. And they told him so. We lived a living hell for five years. And I think Doug survived it pretty good. I really do. He's my hero. 'Course, I'll have to say this. Wade Knox is a hero. He came forth. He is the one that really nailed Jack. But in his own way, he's suffering, too.

"That's where Jack messed up," Hogan continued. "The other boys were molested when they were young. He made a terrible mistake picking on Doug to start with. But see, Doug had age on him, that the other boys didn't have; he was sixteen."

The interviewer said, "He knew what was right and wrong."

"Right. And he was physically large enough to challenge Jack. And he did so. And I think that's the only thing that saved my son."

Thinking back to the night when Jack Walls came into her kitchen to suggest that Joe and Barbara Stocks were abusing Heath, Karen Knox now believes, "He was setting us up. Because he knew what he was doing. He was over there planning Joe and Barbara and Heather's funeral with Heath. This mind thing. This mind thing that he's got going with these kids. It's horrible."

She went on. "The Hogans had a name for suing people, was what we were told. So that's what Jack told everybody, that's what everybody believed. Because the Wallses were the Wallses. I've learned a very important lesson there: you don't judge people like that. You don't take somebody else's word for it. You get out and find out what they're like yourself. I've learned a very important lesson. Name means nothing. It's what your heart is, it's what you are inside."

There was no real breakthrough, no miracle cure for Wade Knox, whose behavior grew more unsteady and disturbed. Paranoid and increasingly dangerous to others and himself, he spent the better part of many nights huddling wide awake in the dark in the Knox house, peering through windows, looking for people who'd come to kill him. Charlie and Karen Knox were mindful that the prosecutor's office had alerted them that there was a very real possibility that they might have been on Jack Walls's hit list, scheduled to be the next to die.

One afternoon, Wade Knox lost it, totally lost it, scaring his parents so badly that they called the police, who came and took him to the state hospital. (Barbara and Joe Stocks had been afraid of Heath, too, right before the end.) His parents committed Wade Knox to the hospital to receive extensive psychiatric care. It seemed to have done him some good, maybe, but after he was released, a routine traffic stop for failing to properly signal ended with him being jailed for striking a police officer and fleeing.

Karen Knox wonders, "What are we doing to society? What are we doing to families? What are we doing to ourselves, when we treat our children like this? What's going to happen to our society if we keep on allowing this, and keeping this behind closed doors? And small-town people keep it in the town. And people with power and money can control who finds out and who doesn't. What are we doing to our kids? They're our future, they're our tomorrows. We don't have a tomorrow if we allow this to happen. We don't have one. That's all."

* * *

What of Pam Walls, Jack's wife and mother of his children? Victims' rights advocate Joye Cook said, "I cannot imagine, if it were my husband, that I would not suspect that something was strange with his behavior with these children. I don't know his wife; I never met his wife; she never showed up at any of the hearings or sentencings. I can't speak for her. Personally, I cannot imagine that I would not know there was something strange about the man's behavior. If I lived in the house with him and he did the things that we know that he did."

Cledis Hogan opined, "Because she had three daughters, and as long as he liked little boys, well, she didn't have to fear him bothering her daughters."

Pam Walls continued to reside in the same house, sharing a driveway with the Knoxes, to whom she has not spoken a single word in two and a half years. Neither have her daughters.

All the key figures in the tragedy were connected, said Dorothy Stocks, Heath Stocks's grandmother. "This Jack Walls and his wife and his girls—he had three girls—they were friends of Joe and Barbara's family. They were *good* friends. Heather was the very best of friends with one of Jack's daughters. They were in the same grade.

"My heart goes out to all of those victims. One friend of Joe's and Barbara's was the Knox family. Lord, Charlie was like a son of mine when they were going to school; they were in the same grade. And I just feel so sorry for the trouble that they're having today. I don't think it'll ever end. None of it. None of it's going to ever end."

Her husband, Martin, had died in the interim, going to the grave without forgiving his grandson for the murders, but Dorothy Stocks said that her faith had helped her to find forgiveness. She visits Heath Stocks at the prison every Wednesday.

She said, "I would like to see Heath's sentence for prison lowered. I've got sense enough to know that Heath has to pay for what he did. But I would like to see the sentence lowered to where someday, Heath could get out. He needs help, and he's not going to get it where he is."

Heath Stocks said that he told his public defender about Jack Walls's influence in the murders. The public defender denies it. Prosecutor Betty Dickey has said, "We believe the public defender knew that Jack was involved, and just let him [Stocks] plead guilty for three lives and be done with it." She has written a letter to the governor asking that this be weighed in regard to possibly reconsidering Heath Stocks's three life sentences.

Jon Johnson, Walls's attorney, said flat-out, "Chances are, Jack's probably going to die in prison." Heath Stocks and many others disagree, believing that Walls will someday be released from prison—someday soon, perhaps. Stocks said, "He's going to get out, more'n likely."

The interviewer asked, "Why?"

"Money and politics. What makes the world go round."

HORRIFYING TRUE CRIME
FROM PINNACLE BOOKS

__No Safe Place
  by Bill G. Cox   0-7860-1037-1 $6.50US/$8.50CAN

__Deacon of Death
  by Fred Rosen   0-7860-1094-0 $6.50US/$8.50CAN

__Die for Me
  by Don Lasseter   0-7860-1107-6 $6.50US/$8.50CAN

__Murder in the Family
  by Burl Barer   0-7860-1135-1 $6.50US/$7.50CAN

__Damaged Goods
  by Jim Henderson   0-7680-1147-5 $6.50US/$8.50CAN

__Driven to Kill
  by Gary C. King   0-7860-1347-8 $6.50US/$8.50CAN

Call toll free **1-888-345-BOOK** to order by phone or use this coupon
to order by mail.

Name_____

Address_____

City_____ State_____ Zip_____

Please send me the books that I checked above.

I am enclosing $_____
Plus postage and handling* $_____
Sales tax (in NY, TN, and DC) $_____
Total amount enclosed $_____

*Add $2.50 for the first book and $.50 for each additional book.

Send check or money order (no cash or CODs) to: **Kensington Publishing
Corp., Dept. C.O., 850 Third Avenue, 16th Floor, New York, NY 10022**

Prices and numbers subject to change without notice.

All orders subject to availability.

Visit our website at **www.kensingtonbooks.com.**